OCCASIONAL PAPER

How Is Deployment to Iraq and Afghanistan Affecting U.S. Service Members and Their Families?

An Overview of Early RAND Research on the Topic

James Hosek, Editor

Prepared for the Office of the Secretary of Defense
Approved for public release; distribution unlimited

RAND NATIONAL DEFENSE RESEARCH INSTITUTE

The research reported here was sponsored by the Office of the Secretary of Defense (OSD). The research was conducted jointly by the Center for Military Health Policy Research, a RAND Health program, and the Forces and Resources Policy Center, a RAND National Defense Research Institute (NDRI) program. NDRI is a federally funded research and development center sponsored by OSD, the Joint Staff, the Unified Combatant Commands, the Navy, the Marine Corps, the defense agencies, and the defense Intelligence Community under Contract W74V8H-06-C-0002.

Library of Congress Cataloging-in-Publication Data

Hosek, James R.
How is deployment to Iraq and Afghanistan affecting U.S. service members and their families? : an overview of early RAND research on the topic / James Hosek.
p. cm.
Includes bibliographical references.
ISBN 978-0-8330-5201-8 (pbk. : alk. paper)
1. Psychology, Military. 2. Iraq War, 2003---Psychological aspects. 3. Afghan War, 2001---Psychological aspects. 4. Deployment (Strategy)—Psychological aspects. 5. Soldiers–Mental health—United States. 6. United States—Armed Forces—Personnel management. 7. United States—Armed Forces—Recruiting, enlistment, etc. 8. Families of military personnel—Services for—United States. I. Title.

U22.3.H67 2011
956.7044'34—dc22

2011005158

Cover photo by Staff Sgt. Ryan C. Matson, courtesy of the United States Army

Published 2011 by the RAND Corporation
1776 Main Street, P.O. Box 2138, Santa Monica, CA 90407-2138
1200 South Hayes Street, Arlington, VA 22202-5050
4570 Fifth Avenue, Suite 600, Pittsburgh, PA 15213-2665
RAND URL: http://www.rand.org/
To order RAND documents or to obtain additional information, contact
Distribution Services: Telephone: (310) 451-7002;
Fax: (310) 451-6915; Email: order@rand.org

Preface

The extended wars in Iraq and Afghanistan over the past decade have affected the lives of approximately two million U.S. service members and their families in many different ways. In an all-volunteer force, the nature of those effects warrants proper attention, because the well-being of troops and the people close to them is a central concern. On one side, it affects military readiness and the ability of the U.S. armed forces to carry out their mission. On the other, it is something the nation has committed itself to in appreciation of the sacrifices made by military families.

Effective policies to facilitate the well-being of this community require a comprehensive understanding of the myriad issues and consequences that service members and their families may face due to the stress of deployment. Yet for much of the 2000s, such understanding was largely lacking. Recognizing the need for analysis, around 2005, the RAND Corporation launched a program of research designed to investigate this theme and, where possible, offer policymakers informed recommendations. This occasional paper introduces this body of work—ongoing today—by presenting an overview of six of the earliest RAND studies on various aspects of the theme. It calls attention to the pressing policy questions, summarizes the key findings and policy implications, and, where applicable, lays out recommendations.

The research described in this paper will be of interest to policymakers, analysts, staff of the U.S. Department of Defense, members of the military community, the service providers who work with and for them, and readers generally concerned with how current military operations are affecting U.S. troops and their families.

The six studies summarized here were conducted within two centers at RAND. The first is the Forces and Resources Policy Center of the RAND National Defense Research Institute. This is a federally funded research and development center sponsored by the Office of the Secretary of Defense, the Joint Staff, the Unified Combatant Commands, the Navy, the Marine Corps, the defense agencies, and the defense Intelligence Community. The second is RAND Health's Center for Military Health Policy Research. This center taps RAND expertise in both defense and health policy to conduct research for the Department of Defense, the Veterans Administration, and nonprofit organizations. RAND Health aims to transform the well-being of all people by solving complex problems in health and health care.

For more information on the Forces and Resources Policy Center, see http://www.rand.org/nsrd/about/frp.html or contact the director (contact information is provided on the web page). For more information on the Center for Military Health Policy Research, see http://www.rand.org/multi/military.html or contact the co-directors (contact information is provided on the web page).

Contents

Figures

Acknowledgments

The authors of the documents summarized in this paper sincerely wish to thank RAND colleague Susan Bohandy for her role in preparing the summaries.

1. Introduction

The conflicts in Iraq and Afghanistan have put the all-volunteer force to its most severe test since its inception in 1973. Of all of the wars the United States has fought to date, Afghanistan is the second longest, with Iraq taking a close third place—both superseded only by Vietnam. In this environment of ongoing demand for battle-ready soldiers, sailors, airmen, and marines, concerns are growing about the effects and consequences of prolonged stress on the force as a whole, and on individual service members and their families. Among the concerns are questions about the resilience of the all-volunteer force, potential earnings losses of activated reservists, the nature of battlefield casualties, the care service members receive if wounded, and the emotional health of the children of deployed parents.

Over the past five years, the RAND Corporation has produced a diverse body of research that offers insight into these issues. These studies were among the first to take up the theme of how deployments to Iraq and Afghanistan are affecting service members and their families, and to offer policymakers informed recommendations. The earliest study, reported in *Stress and Performance*, was completed in 2005 (Kavanagh, 2005). It took a detailed look at how the acute stress of today's military deployments might alter the performance of service members in the theater. *Activation and the Earnings of Reservists* (Loughran, Klerman, and Martin, 2006) followed in 2006, describing an investigation of whether deployment led to a loss of income for reservists while away from their civilian jobs. The year 2008 saw the publication of two reports: *Invisible Wounds of War* (Tanielian and Jaycox, 2008), based on a comprehensive study of the psychological and cognitive injuries of deployed service members, and *Deployment Experiences of Guard and Reserve Families* (Castaneda et al., 2008), based on a study that probed the unique experience of families of activated guardsmen and reservists. In 2009, RAND released *How Have Deployments During the War on Terrorism Affected Reenlistment?* (Hosek and Martorell, 2009). This study, which included an analysis of actual reenlistment behavior and expanded on an earlier study based on focus groups and data on intentions (*How Deployments Affect Service Members*, Hosek, Kavanagh, and Miller, 2006), examined whether current deployments were negatively affecting reenlistment rates within the four services. "Children on the Homefront: The Experience of Children from Military Families," published as a journal article in early 2010 (Chandra et al., 2010), reported on a study of the issues faced by children of a deployed parent while that parent is absent and after he or she returns.

These six studies sparked the development of a rich body of research that continues to grow. Some of the study results and recommendations are no longer new, but they have nonetheless laid important groundwork and set the direction for newer studies being carried out today. This paper brings the research together in an abridged form, highlighting the policy questions, key findings, and policy implications.

2. How Has Deployment Affected Reenlistment?

Hosek and Martorell, 2009: *How Have Deployments During the War on Terrorism Affected Reenlistment?*

More than 1.7 million U.S. service members have been deployed since 2002 for Operation Iraqi Freedom (OIF) in Iraq and Operation Enduring Freedom (OEF) in Afghanistan. During the invasion of Iraq in 2003, the number of troops in the two theaters jumped to nearly 300,000, and the monthly count of service members deployed since then for hostile duty—including those in other theaters—has ranged from 150,000 to 200,000 (Figure 2.1). The operations have been manned on a rotational basis. This approach spreads deployments over the entire pool of deployable service members. But because the Iraq and Afghanistan operations have been so lengthy, there have been multiple deployments for many personnel, especially soldiers and marines. Army and Marine units, and unit members, have also deployed more frequently

Figure 2.1
Number of U.S. Service Members Deployed, 1996–2007

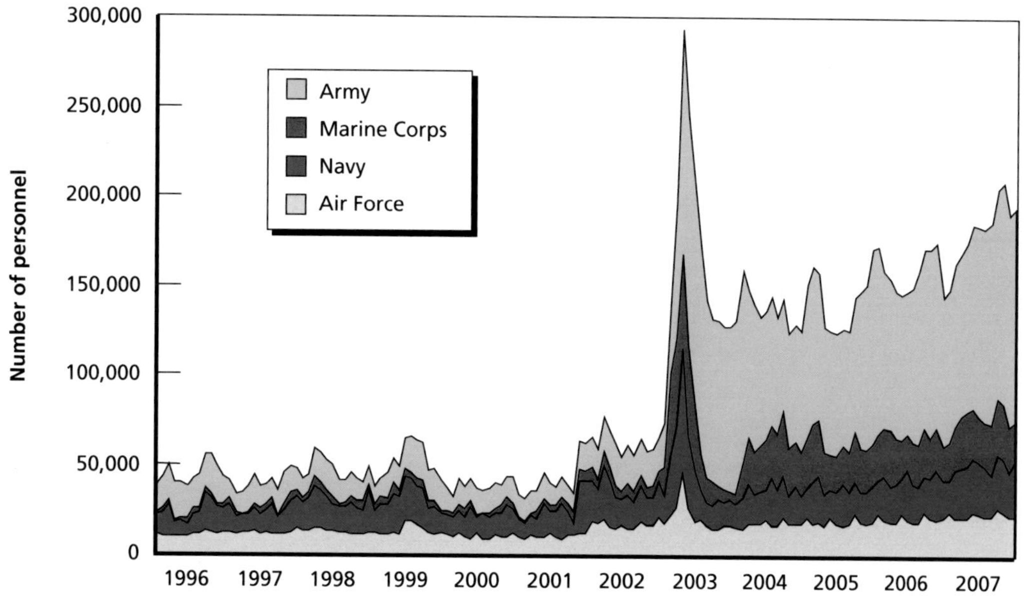

RAND *OP316-2.1*

than planned, and have had less time between deployments to recuperate, regenerate, and train and exercise for the next deployment. In addition, most personnel have been exposed to combat or imminent danger while deployed. Long hours, poor living conditions in the theater, and limited communications with families compound these stresses.

A key question has been whether the demanding tempo of deployments has caused reenlistment rates to decrease. A drop in first- and second-term reenlistment rates would mean the loss of trained, experienced personnel and greater turbulence in unit manning. At the same time, to offset the higher outflow of personnel, an increase in recruitment and training would be needed.

This study focused on a period starting in 1996, before the conflicts in Afghanistan and Iraq erupted, and ending in 2007. The RAND study team used econometric modeling to estimate how deployment to a hostile environment affected service members' decision to reenlist. Deployment is one of many factors influencing the reenlistment decision, and the models in the analysis control for the effects of other factors.[1]

The study used two data sets, each with different information on service members. The first contained survey data from ten "Status of Forces Surveys of Active Duty Personnel" conducted between 2002 and 2005. These surveys asked active-duty personnel about such issues as work-related and personal stress, intention to stay in the military, number of days worked that were longer than the usual duty day, whether deployment was longer or shorter than expected, and individual preparedness for the missions to be undertaken. The second data set comprised administrative files on pay and personnel that spanned the 11 years from 1996 to 2007.

RAND received permission to link these two data sets. This offered the advantage of showing whether intentions to stay in the military were borne out by subsequent reenlistment decisions. However, the administrative data—which covered all active-duty enlisted personnel and included all reenlist/leave decisions for the 1996–2007 period—afforded the most-detailed insights into the relationship between deployment and reenlistment.

How Has Deployment Affected Work Stress, Personal Stress, and the Intention to Stay in the Military?

In the Status of Forces surveys, respondents were asked whether their levels of work-related and personal stress were higher or lower than usual. The study's analysis estimated whether an individual's reported stress levels, as well as his or her intention to stay in the military, were affected by having been deployed within the 12 months prior to taking the survey. Soldiers, sailors, and marines who had been deployed were more likely to report higher-than-usual work stress and higher-than-usual personal stress. The sizes of these effects were quite similar at first- and second-term reenlistments; Figure 2.2 shows the results at first term. Deployment had a particularly strong effect on work-related stress among soldiers. In contrast, the effects on airmen were near zero—that is, deployment did not elevate self-reported stress for deployed airmen relative to the levels for airmen who did not deploy.

---

[1] Branch of service, occupational specialty, marital status, race/ethnicity, gender, education, Armed Forces Qualification Test (AFQT) score, years of service, term of service, nature of deployments (i.e., hostile or non-hostile), fast promotion, and reenlistment bonus may also play a role.

Figure 2.2
Effect of Deployment on Work and Personal Stress, First Term, by Service

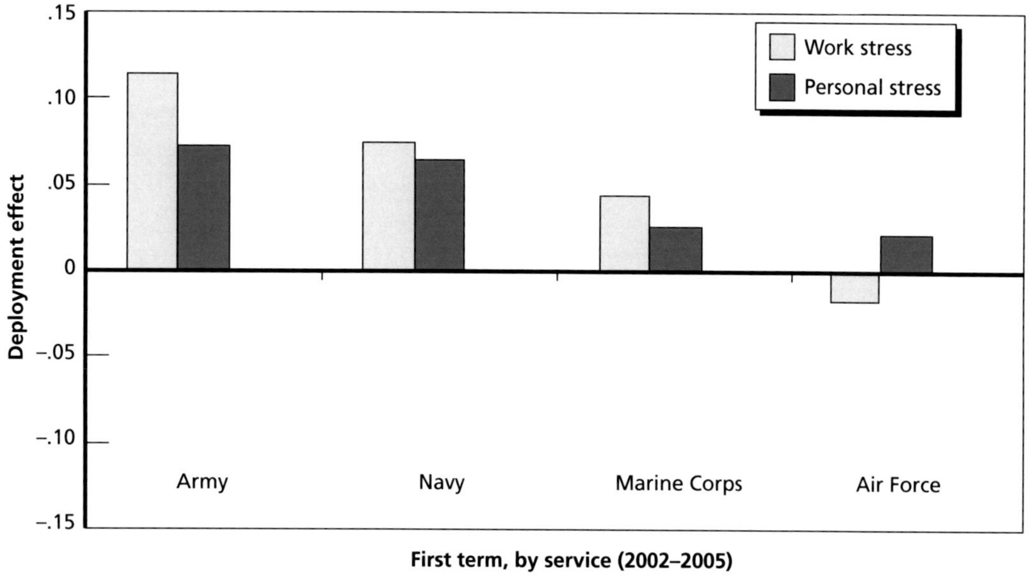

RAND *OP316-2.2*

At the same time, deployment decreased the intention to reenlist at first term in all services, with the effect being strongest among soldiers and marines (Figure 2.3). At second term, deployment's effect on the intention to reenlist was negative and smaller in size (closer to zero) for the Army and Air Force, and zero for the Navy and Marine Corps. This difference in deployment effects between first- and second-term is consistent with findings in past research

Figure 2.3
Effect of Deployment on the Intention to Reenlist, First Term, by Service

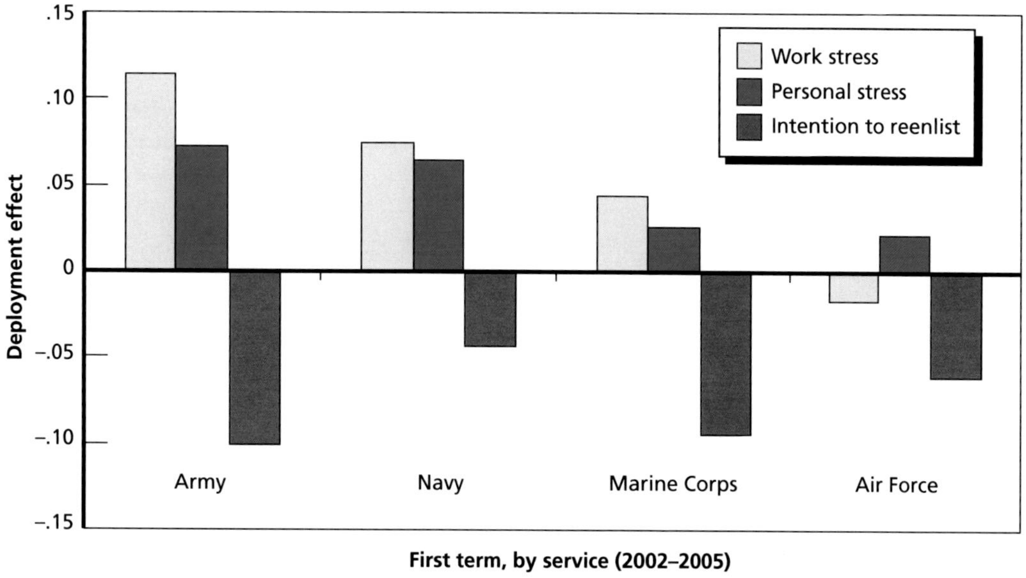

RAND *OP316-2.3*

and probably results from the selective nature of reenlistment: Those with more tolerance for deployment are more likely to remain in the military at the first-term reenlistment decision point, other things being equal.

By linking the survey data to administrative data, the RAND analysts could determine whether service members followed through on their intentions. There was a strong tendency to do so at first term: Those personnel who as a consequence of deployment said they were "less likely" or "much less likely" to reenlist, in fact, had a lower probability of reenlisting. But the effects of deployment on actual reenlistment were considerably smaller than the effects on the intention to reenlist (half the size or less).

At the second term, though, intentions were not consistent with behavior. The effects of deployment on actual reenlistment at that time were zero in the Army and Air Force, even though deployment had a negative effect on the intentions of soldiers and airmen. In the Navy and Marine Corps, the effects of deployment on actual reenlistment were positive, but zero when it came to intentions to reenlist. The clear implication of the first- and second-term findings was that the effect of deployment on intentions to reenlist, stated at the time of the survey, underestimated the effect of deployment on subsequent actual reenlistment.

The Status of Forces survey provided other insights on how service members react to aspects of deployment. There were several key findings:

- The survey data included the number of days respondents had served in the previous year that were longer than the usual duty day. The inclusion of this variable in the analysis typically shifted toward zero the effect that deployment had on each of the dependent variables (higher-than-usual work stress, higher-than-usual personal stress, intention to stay, and actual reenlistment). The implication is that much of what underlies the effect of "deployment" has to do with the number of long workdays. This is not to discount the possible role of specific dangers such as improvised explosive devices (IEDs), snipers, ambushes, and other hazards. But available data sets do not contain variables on these factors.
- Deployments that were either much shorter or much longer than expected decreased the intention to stay in the military. This finding implies that service members feel discontent when reality turns out to be much different than expected and suggests the importance of setting accurate expectations about the length of a deployment. This is consistent with the view that service members prefer accurate, certain expectations to inaccurate or uncertain ones: They prefer to know when the deployment will occur and how long it will be, and to feel assured that expectations will be met.
- The intention to stay in the military depended on the level of preparedness for the duties performed while deployed. Service members who felt well prepared were more likely to state a positive intention to reenlist.

A Detailed Look at the Effect of Deployment on Reenlistment

The four services fared differently with respect to how deployment affected their personnel. Making use of the extensive administrative data, the RAND researchers first explored models with an indicator for whether the service member had been deployed in the year prior to the reenlistment decision. The effect of this deployment variable was allowed to vary by year, and separate models were estimated for first- and second-term personnel by branch of service. The advantage of this approach was that it could detect possible time trends in the effect of deployment. For deployment involving hostile duty or imminent danger, the most dramatic trends were in the Army (Figure 2.4). For both first- and second-term Army reenlistment, the effect of deployment was initially positive in 1996 and had a slight downward trend till 2004. The effect then plummeted from a positive value in 2004 to a negative value in 2006. Analysis of subgroups added nuance to these findings but repeated the same pattern:

- The effects of deployment were similar for men and women soldiers during the first years of OIF and OEF (and before). But the negative effect in 2006–2007 was stronger for men. This was true at both first- and second-term reenlistment.
- In any year during the two operations, the effect of deployment on reenlistment was less positive or more negative for soldiers in combat arms occupational specialties than for those not in combat arms specialties. In 2006, the effect in non-combat arms was to reduce first-term reenlistment by 7 percentage points (relative to soldiers who had no hostile deployment), while the effect in combat arms was to reduce reenlistment by 14 percentage points. The 2006 effects at second-term reenlistment were practically identical. These findings represent large impacts on reenlistment rates that were, on average, about 35 percent at first term and about 60 percent at second term. The more-pronounced negative effects among soldiers in combat arms seem likely to be associated with greater exposure to combat-related traumatic events.

Figure 2.4
Effect of Deployment on Army Reenlistment for Hostile Deployment in 12 Months Prior to Reenlistment Decision, by Year

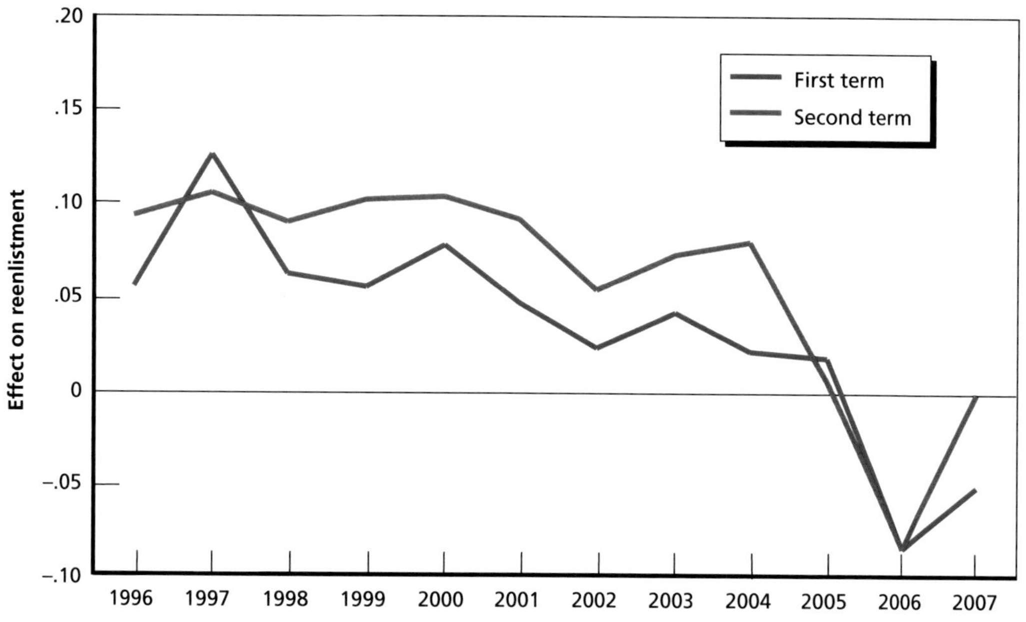

RAND *OP316-2.4*

- Deployment effects differed little with respect to marital status at first term. But at second term, the deployment effects were 2 to 3 percentage points lower for single personnel than for married, and this held true throughout the 1996–2007 period.

This raised an important question: Why had the Army experienced this sharp reversal in deployment's effect on reenlistment when the other services had not? The results for the Navy, Marine Corps, and Air Force showed that the effect of deployment on first-term reenlistment was small—with near-zero values from 1996 to 2007—and that the effect on second-term reenlistment was about zero in 2003 and tended to increase from 2003 to 2007, years of heavy involvement in Iraq and Afghanistan.[2]

The cause of this particular trend in the Army appears to be a combination of two factors. First, the effect of deployment varied with the *cumulative* months of deployment in the three years before the reenlistment decision. Second, as a result of the rapid pace and high level of Army deployments, many soldiers had a large number of cumulative months of deployment.

Cumulative deployment was coded into variables reflecting one to six months, seven to 11 months, 12 to 17 months, and 18 or more months, with zero months being the base group. The effect of one to six months of deployment was positive and increasing after 2002, the effect of seven to 11 months was near zero, the effect of 12 to 17 months was negative and decreasing after 2002, and the effect of 18 or more months was still lower and tending to decrease after 2002 (Figure 2.5). In short, the effect of deployment for soldiers with 12 or more months of deployment was negative.

The Marine Corps results were not as clear-cut as the Army's, but from 2004 onward, the effects of seven or more months of deployment (i.e., seven to 11, 12 to 17, and 18 or more months) were all negative with two exceptions: 12 to 17 months in 2006 and 2007. To put the Army and Marine Corps results in context, note that Army deployments to OIF/OEF were 12 to 15 months, whereas Marine Corps deployments were typically seven months. Thus, high months of deployment also had a negative effect on reenlistment in the Marine Corps.

In 2006, 79 percent of the soldiers at first-term reenlistment had had some hostile deployment; and of those deployed, two-thirds had 12 or more cumulative months, and nearly 20 percent had 18 or more cumulative months (Figure 2.6). The Marine Corps had 80 percent of marines with some deployment, 44 percent of whom had 12 or more months, and 6 percent of whom had 18 or more months. Cumulative months of deployment were much lower within the other services. The Navy had 68 percent with some deployment, 3 percent of whom had 12 or more months, and the numbers for the Air Force were 48 percent, 11 percent of whom had 12 or more months.

Putting the findings together led to the conclusion that the sharp fall from positive to negative in deployment's effect on Army reenlistment from 2004 to 2006 most likely was the product of the negative effect on reenlistment for soldiers with high numbers of months of deployment and the high percentage of soldiers who by then had accumulated high numbers of months of deployment. Similar findings for the Marine Corps indicate that for it, too, deployment had a decreasing effect on reenlistment, though that effect did not become negative.

---

[2] There was a downward trend in the effect of deployment on second-term reenlistment in the Navy and Marine Corps from 1998 to 2003. The cause of this downward trend is not known.

Figure 2.5
Effect of Soldiers' Cumulative Months of Hostile Deployment on Reenlistment, 1996–2007

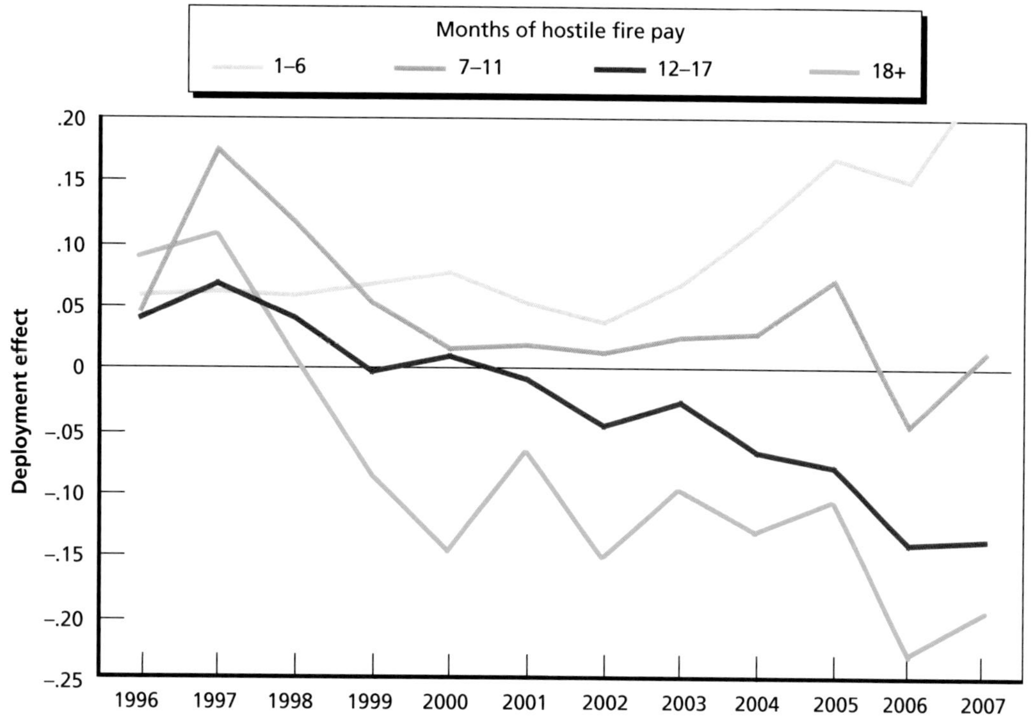

RAND *OP316-2.5*

Counteracting the Negative Effect of Cumulative Deployment on Army Reenlistment in 2006 and 2007

Cumulative deployment's negative effect on Army reenlistment and decreasing effect on Marine Corps reenlistment would have been entirely hidden to policymakers looking only at overall reenlistment rates. Virtually none of the duress from deployment would have been apparent, as reenlistment rates for each of the services held fairly steady over the 1996–2007 period, even during the years following 9/11. This point is illustrated by first-term reenlistment rates (Figure 2.7) and also holds for second-term rates.

The study found that a major reason for overall stable reenlistment rates was the aggressive use of reenlistment bonuses. At the same time as the deployment burden on soldiers rose so rapidly, the Army significantly expanded the number of occupations eligible for a reenlistment bonus and increased the dollar amount of those bonuses (Figure 2.8). The percentage of reenlisting soldiers who received a bonus increased from 15 percent in 2003–2004 to nearly 80 percent in 2005–2007, while the average value of bonuses increased by more than 50 percent. Interestingly, the expanded use of bonuses began in 2005, before the negative effect of deployment on reenlistment had been detected. It was in response to orders to increase the size of the Army and provide bonuses to troops who reenlisted when deployed, regardless of whether their occupational specialty was designated as a critical skill. The Army increased its

Figure 2.6
Cumulative Months of Hostile Deployment in the Army, 1996–2007

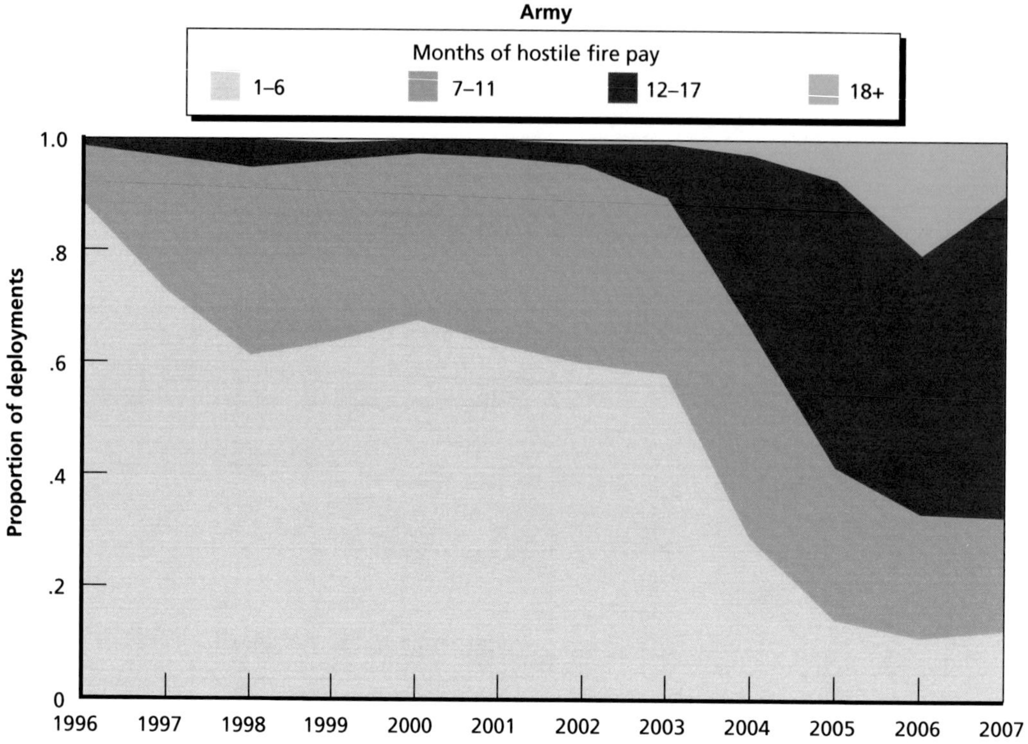

RAND *OP316-2.6*

Figure 2.7
First-Term Reenlistment by Service, 1996–2007

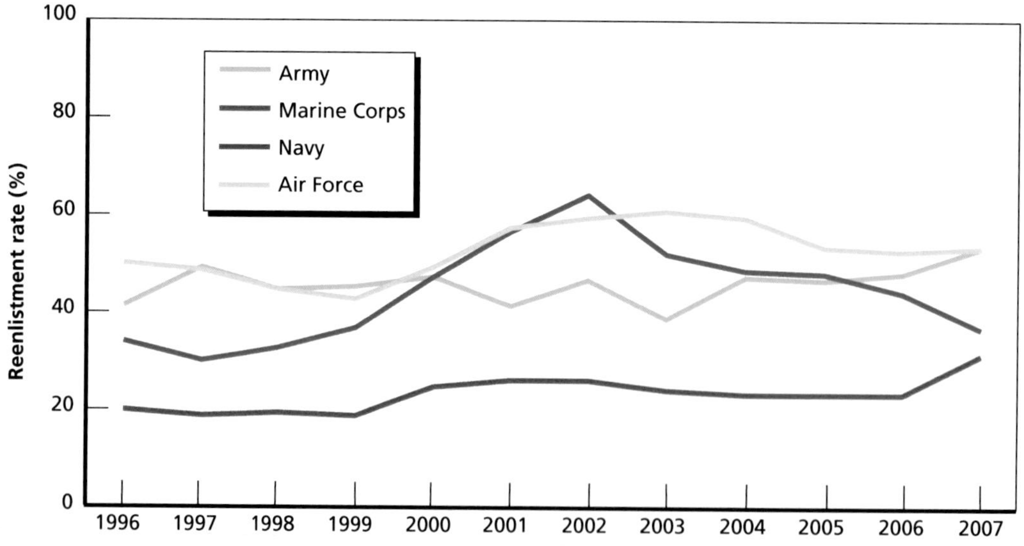

RAND *OP316-2.7*

Figure 2.8
Percentage of Reenlisting First-Term Soldiers Receiving Bonuses and Bonus Amounts, 1996–2007

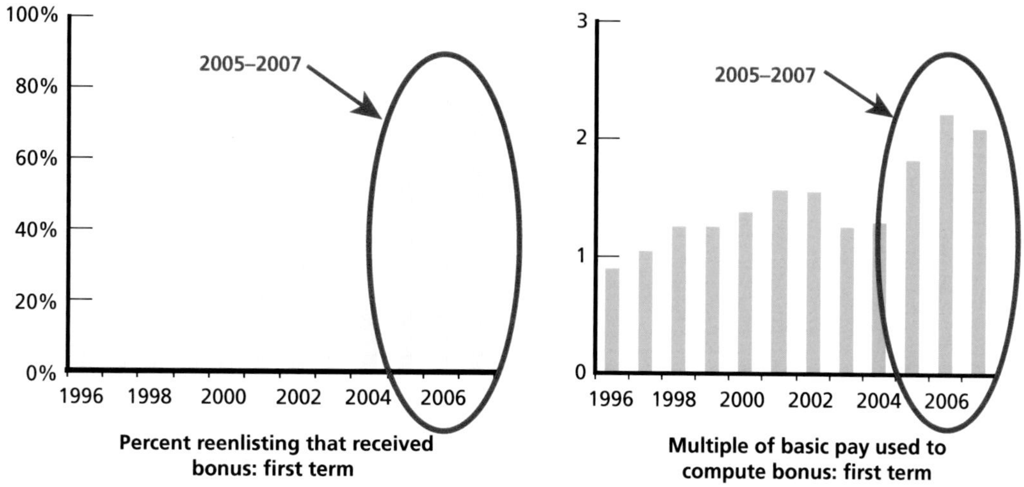

RAND *OP316-2.8*

recruiting and retention targets, allocated more recruiting resources, and greatly increased its use of enlistment and reenlistment bonuses. This expansion in reenlistment bonuses was fortuitous in the sense that the bonuses helped to stave off a decrease in reenlistment from deployment in 2006 and 2007. The Marine Corps, also under orders to grow, similarly expanded its enlistment and reenlistment bonus offerings. Like the Army, it met its growth targets while preventing any decrease in reenlistment.

AREAS FOR FURTHER STUDY

- Whether longer versus shorter deployments and more-prolonged exposure to combat lead to lower reenlistment rates and a higher prevalence of mental health conditions.
- What can be done to avoid either of those outcomes, if either is indeed found to be a cost of longer deployments.
- What factors other than bonuses may have played a role in keeping Army reenlistment rates steady—e.g., better communication links between deployed soldiers and their families, improved family support programs, and training focused on what to expect during a deployment (such as the Army's Battlemind training program).
- How deployment affects retention in the reserves.

3. The Consequences of Combat Stress in Iraq and Afghanistan: Effects on Troop Performance

Kavanagh, 2005: *Stress and Performance, A Review of the Literature and Its Applicability to the Military*

Stress has always been a reality of warfare, and the wars in Iraq and Afghanistan have been no exception. In a 2003 survey of soldiers and marines serving in Iraq, 89 percent of soldiers and 95 percent of marines reported having been attacked or ambushed. Nearly 100 percent of both groups surveyed had been shot at or had received small-arms fire. Although these percentages were lower in Afghanistan at that time, they were still striking: 58 percent of Army personnel, for example, had been attacked or ambushed, and 66 percent had been shot at or received small-arms fire. The recent expansion of operations in Afghanistan can be expected to have raised these percentages in that theater.

U.S. combat troops in both countries have had to cope with a variety of traumatic events (Figure 3.1), including roadside bombs, improvised explosive devices (IEDs), suicide bombers, and a host of other stressful experiences unique to the urban combat type of warfare that characterizes these conflicts.[1] Some have had to kill enemy combatants and handle human remains. They have seen their fellow soldiers and friends dead and injured and have often felt helpless to stop violent situations (Hoge et al., 2004). Strenuous deployment schedules with little rest in between tours only add to the stress.

With service members exposed to such high and ongoing levels of stress in the two theaters, both the military and the public have turned their attention to the possible consequences. One concern is performance: Does the intense stress of ground operations in Iraq and Afghanistan affect the performance of troops and, if so, in what ways?

As a professional fighting force, the all-volunteer military depends on service members performing at their best. Mistakes and bad decisions can lead not only to failed missions, but also to unnecessary casualties on both sides and among civilians. A 1985 study found that battle fatigue and other stress reactions may account for as many as 50 percent of the casualties in a given war (Mareth and Brooker, 1985). Protective gear and sophisticated weapons can do much to enhance the performance of U.S. troops and keep people out of harm's way, but human error remains a decisive factor.

[1] Examples include close quarters, intense firefights, obstructed visibility due to tall buildings, an unidentified and constantly changing enemy, and unforeseen obstacles.

Figure 3.1
Traumatic Events Experienced by Troops in Afghanistan and Iraq

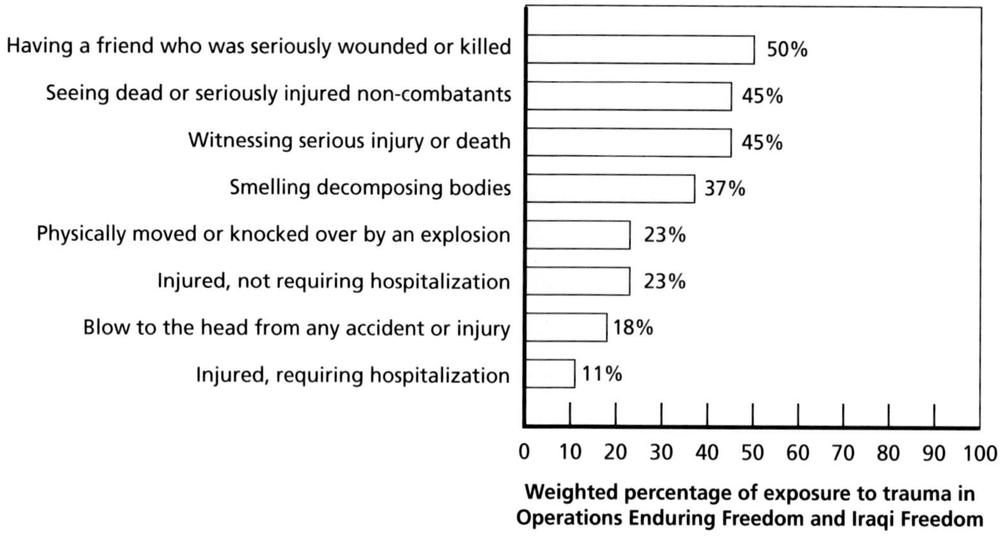

SOURCE: April 2008 RAND briefing based on research for Tanielian and Jaycox, 2008.
RAND *OP316-3.1*

This RAND study mined a wealth of existing research on the relationship between stress and performance to investigate how that relationship may play out specifically in the military context. It also identified ways in which general techniques for moderating the effects of stress can be adapted for military purposes.

Performance May Suffer When Individuals Are Under Stress

Humans come under stress when they are exposed to demanding events or stimuli, referred to as *stressors* in technical literature and scientific research. Lack of sleep, extreme temperatures, time pressure, and physical assault are all examples. In a military theater, stressors can include the many traumatic experiences that soldiers and marines serving in Iraq and Afghanistan have reported in surveys.

Regardless of their form, stressors produce similar, measurable physiological responses in the human body, such as elevated heart rate, dilated pupils, and increased blood pressure. These responses are at least partially adaptive, in that they prepare the body to function effectively in challenging circumstances. But this adaptive response can also have significant downsides if the physiological changes negatively affect performance (Figure 3.2 provides examples).

When an individual experiences stress, his or her cognitive performance and decision-making may be adversely affected. The person may screen out peripheral stimuli and lose the ability to process information and analyze complicated situations. When this happens, thinking narrows and the person is likely to use rigid or narrow rules of thumb and mental shortcuts rather than informed evaluation to guide his or her actions. It may take the person longer to complete a task or reduce the accuracy of the performance. Group functioning may also suffer—researchers have found a higher incidence of groupthink, less effective communication, and a greater tendency to defer control to superiors within groups under stress.

Figure 3.2
Progression from Stressors to Negative Effects on Performance

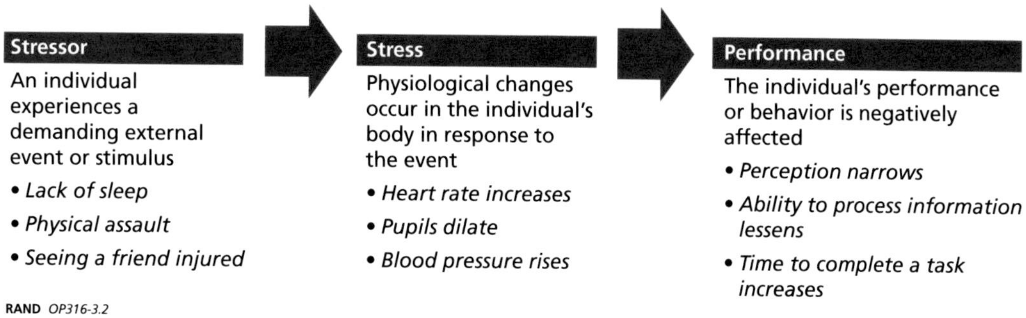

RAND *OP316-3.2*

Is Stress Always Bad? Finding the Right Balance Between Too Much and Too Little

But while sustained exposure to severe stressors has negative effects on mental processing and performance, extensive research shows that stress in moderate doses may actually enhance performance.

The relationship between stress and performance can be envisioned as an upside-down U shape (Figure 3.3). At the top of this shape, performance is optimal: Stress causes enough stimulation to keep an individual vigilant and alert, but not so much that the body's physiological responses impede concentration, analysis, and accuracy. At the side of the inverted U's base where there is little or no stress, however, alertness and engagement may be too low for an individual to perform effectively. And at the other side of the base, where there is extreme

Figure 3.3
Relationship Between Stress and the Quality of Performance

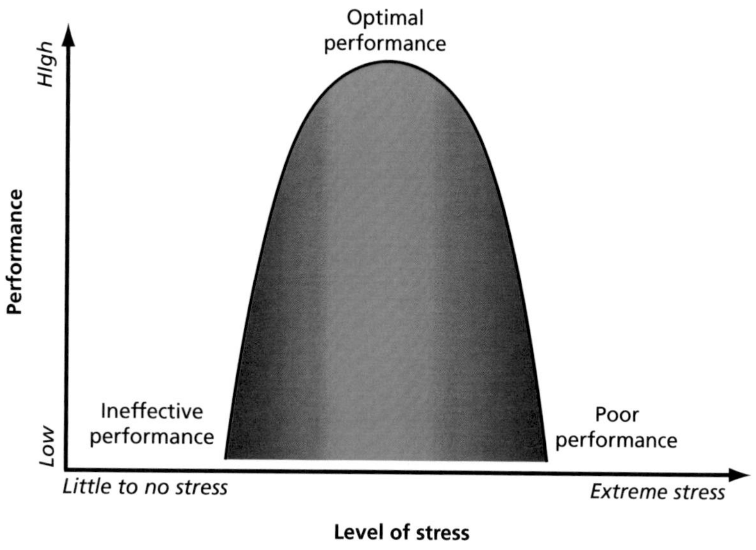

RAND *OP316-3.3*

stress (which can be in the form of either extended exposure to a set of stressors or a single exposure to one intense stressor), arousal may be high enough to prevent an individual from performing well.

In the military context, troops may perform optimally when engaged in operations and activities with moderate stress levels. When stress levels are too low, boredom and low arousal may cause performance to deteriorate, possibly jeopardizing an operation's success. And operations that involve very high or sustained stress levels (or both) may present especially significant challenges to military personnel and planners.

The Military Can Use Training and Other Moderators to Reduce the Negative Effects of Stress

Techniques that strengthen service members' ability to cope with elevated and constant stress levels may prevent performance from suffering in these contexts. One way to minimize the negative performance effects of severe stress is to take advantage of *moderators*—i.e., factors that intervene in the relationship between stress and performance, in most cases reducing stress's negative effects. Moderators fall into two categories (Figure 3.4): factors that moderate an individual's response to a stressor and factors that moderate the effects of stress on performance.[2]

Training is the most important moderator in the military context. It is proven not only to reduce the effect of stressors on the body's physiological response (i.e., stress), but also to

Figure 3.4
Two Categories of Moderators That Lessen the Negative Effects of Stress on Performance

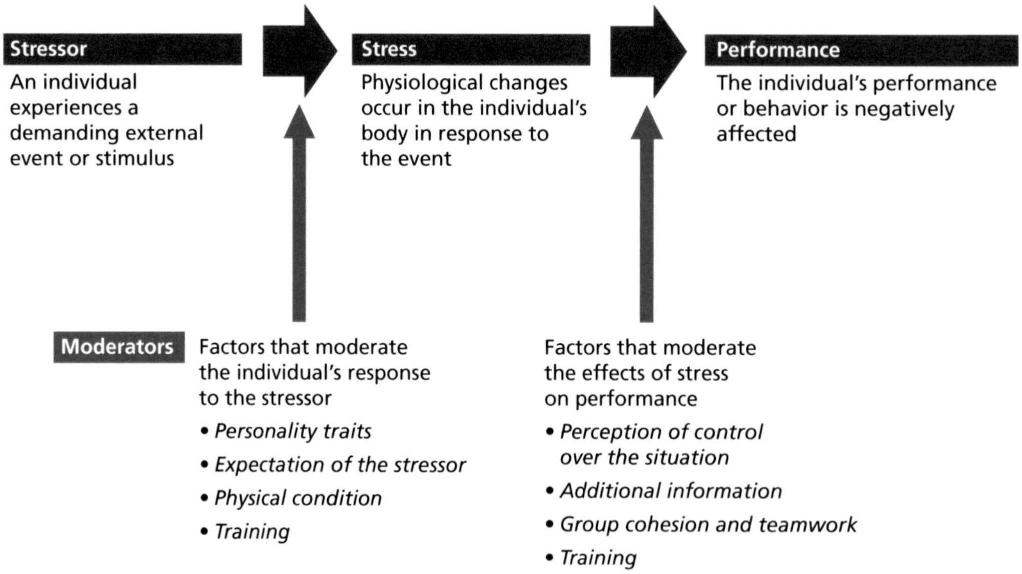

RAND *OP316-3.4*

[2] In addition to moderators, treatment and therapy can be effective ways to help reduce the adverse effects of stress on functioning.

mitigate the consequent effects of stress on performance. Stress exposure training is particularly promising for military use, with both individual service members and units. Participants are exposed to simulated stressors they are likely to encounter in combat and then made to perform target skills while under stress. Studies have shown that for military personnel, this sort of prior exposure to deployment-like situations and challenges reduces uncertainty and improves performance in the theater. It familiarizes participants with potential stressors and their effects, creates more-accurate expectations, teaches strategies for maintaining performance under stress, and builds self-confidence. Among groups, it enhances communication, teamwork, and strategies for feedback—all of which facilitate functioning when stressed.

Training Programs Should Follow Several Core Guidelines

Research indicates that providing troops with targeted training programs may be highly effective in helping them maintain performance in new and highly stressful combat zones.[3] These programs should follow several guidelines:

- Realistically represent the environment in which the service member will be expected to perform
- Be targeted to building particular needed skills
- Improve the service member's ability to adapt
- Include adequate feedback from instructors.

The Army and Marine Corps have taken steps in this direction, implementing more advanced training scenarios for soldiers and marines deploying to Iraq and Afghanistan. These scenarios include many aspects of Iraq-like urban combat and living conditions, realistically depicting the environment the service members will confront upon arrival.

AREAS FOR FURTHER STUDY

- How performance is affected when individuals experience multiple stressors (often both physical and emotional) simultaneously.
- How training can be designed to deal with the likely event that service members will experience many stressors at the same time.
- Whether the extensive military training that simulates battlefield conditions, developed over the past decade, has had any effects on military personnel's ability to deal specifically with conflict-related stressors.

[3] Other measures, such as support programs and additional information, might also be helpful, but there has been little systematic study of their content, delivery, and effects.

4. The Invisible Wounds of War: Psychological and Cognitive Injuries Among Veterans of Iraq and Afghanistan

Tanielian and Jaycox, 2008:
Invisible Wounds of War: Psychological and Cognitive Injuries, Their Consequences, and Services to Assist Recovery

Combat operations over the past seven years in Afghanistan and Iraq have been intense, with periods of heavy fighting. Yet the toll of killed and wounded has been dramatically lower than in previous lengthy conflicts. By 2007, the 1.64 million troops that had been deployed to the two theaters had reached half the number of service members (3.4 million) involved in Vietnam. But while nearly 47,500 were killed in action in the eight years of the Vietnam conflict, only 3,500 deaths had been reported in Operations Iraqi and Enduring Freedom by spring 2008, after five years of operations. Similarly, about 153,000 were wounded in Vietnam, whereas approximately 31,000 had been wounded in Iraq and Afghanistan by early 2008. The difference in the ratio of killed to wounded in today's conflicts compared with previous ones is especially striking: For every 2.4 service members wounded in World War II, one died. In Vietnam, that ratio was 3:1. In Afghanistan and Iraq, however, only about one service member has lost his or her life for every nine wounded.

Advanced technology is the principal reason that so many lives are being saved. Not only is the body armor given to all forces in Afghanistan and Iraq vastly improved from that used in previous conflicts, but cutting-edge medical technology is keeping many service members alive who would likely have died before. Wounded troops now receive highly effective emergency medical care in the theater and can be evacuated within 24 hours to a trauma center located in Germany, treated en route in what are essentially "flying intensive care units." In contrast, troops wounded in Vietnam who were being transported for treatment spent approximately 45 days in transit before reaching a U.S. hospital.

But instead of physical injuries and deaths, in today's conflicts another sort of casualty is on the rise. Those service members whose lives are saved by medical technology sometimes suffer significant long-term emotional and cognitive injuries. Moreover, those not directly injured in battle while deployed may still suffer these invisible wounds if exposed to traumatic events or sustained stress.

Safeguarding the psychological health of these service members and veterans is an important part of ensuring the future readiness of the U.S. military forces and fulfilling a commitment to care for those who have served our nation. In the wake of reports and media attention, public concern about the care of the war wounded is high. In 2007, several task forces, independent review groups, and a Presidential Commission examined the care of the war wounded and recommended improvements. Congress, the Department of Defense (DoD), and the Department of Veterans Affairs (VA) responded, making many policy changes and funding shifts to address these issues.

At the time, the impetus for policy change outpaced the knowledge needed to inform solutions. There were fundamental gaps in our understanding of the mental health and cognitive needs of U.S. service members returning from Afghanistan and Iraq, the costs of mental health and cognitive conditions, and the care systems available to deliver treatment.

Understanding Invisible Wounds: The Research Challenge

This comprehensive RAND study of the mental health and cognitive needs of returning service members and veterans began to close these knowledge gaps. RAND researchers focused on three major conditions: posttraumatic stress disorder (PTSD), major depression, and traumatic brain injury (TBI). Unlike physical wounds, these conditions affect mood, thoughts, and behavior and often remain invisible to other service members, family, and society. In addition, symptoms of these conditions, especially PTSD and depression, can have a delayed onset—appearing months after exposure to stress. The effects of TBI are still poorly understood, leaving a large gap in understanding how extensive the problem is or how to address it.

The study addressed questions in three areas:

- *Prevalence:* What are the rates of mental health and cognitive conditions that troops face when returning from deployment to Afghanistan and Iraq?
- *The care system:* What programs and services exist to meet the health care needs of returning troops with PTSD, major depression, or TBI? Where are the gaps in programs and services? What steps can be taken to close the gaps?
- *Costs:* What are the societal costs of these conditions? How much would it cost to deliver high-quality care to all who need it?

To answer these questions, members of the study team undertook a series of research tasks. They reviewed existing scientific research on PTSD, depression, and TBI; surveyed a representative sample of current service members and veterans about their current health status, as well as their access to and use of care; and developed an economic model to estimate the costs associated with these conditions. To identify gaps in access to and quality of care, they also assessed the systems of care designed to provide treatment for these conditions and evaluated what is known about the effectiveness of the services being offered. The study was conducted independently from the DoD and VA and was the first of its kind to take a broad, comprehensive view and to consider these problems.

About One-Third of Returning Service Members Reported Symptoms of a Mental Health or Cognitive Condition

The survey of recently returned service members drew from the population of all those deployed for Operations Enduring Freedom and Iraqi Freedom, regardless of service branch, component, or unit type. The survey used random digit dialing to reach a representative sample within the targeted locations. All participants were guaranteed confidentiality; the survey data were not linked to any individual's government records. A total of 1,965 individuals responded.

Results showed that as of spring 2008:

- 18.5 percent of all returning service members met criteria for either PTSD or depression (see Figure 4.1); 14 percent of all returning service members met criteria for PTSD, and 14 percent met criteria for depression.
- 19.5 percent reported experiencing a probable TBI during their deployment.
- About 7 percent met criteria for a mental health problem and also reported having experienced a possible TBI.

The study estimated that if these numbers are representative, then of the 1.64 million troops deployed as of 2007, approximately 300,000 of those who had returned from Iraq and Afghanistan had a probable disorder of either PTSD or major depression, and about 320,000 may have experienced TBI during deployment.

Many Services Are Available, But the Care Systems Have Gaps

What programs and services exist to meet the needs of returning troops with these conditions? What are the gaps? What steps can be taken to close the gaps? To address these questions, the RAND team examined the care systems, identified gaps in care and barriers to care, and assessed how best to fill these gaps.

Figure 4.1
An Estimated 19 Percent of Troops That Had Returned from Iraq and Afghanistan Had a Mental Health Condition

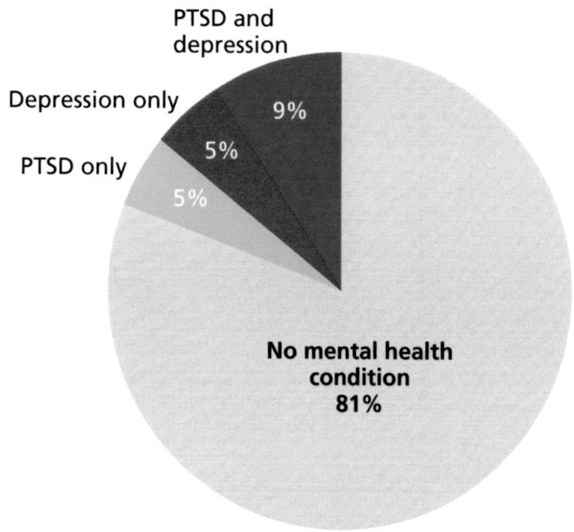

NOTE: Numbers shown have been rounded.
RAND *OP316-4.1*

Access Gaps

In recent years, the capacity of DoD and the VA to provide health services increased substantially, particularly in the areas of mental health and TBI. However, gaps in access and quality remained. In particular, there has been a large gap between the need for mental health services and the use of those services.

This pattern stems from structural factors, such as the availability of providers, as well as from personal, organizational, and cultural factors. For example, military service members reported barriers to seeking care that are associated with fears about the negative consequences of using mental health services. The study's survey results (Figure 4.2) suggested that most of these concerns center on confidentiality and career issues, and so are particularly relevant for those on active duty. Many felt that seeking mental health care might cause career prospects to suffer or coworkers' trust to decline.

However, the VA also faces challenges in providing access to returning service members, who may face long wait times for appointments, particularly in facilities resourced primarily to meet the demands of older veterans. Better projections of the amount and type of demand among newer veterans are needed to ensure that the VA has appropriate resources to meet potential demand.

These access gaps translate into a substantial unmet need for care. The survey found that only 53 percent of returning troops who met criteria for PTSD or major depression had sought help from a provider for these conditions in the past year. The gap was even larger for those reporting a probable TBI: 57 percent had not been evaluated by a physician for a brain injury.

Quality Gaps

The study identified gaps in the delivery of quality care. Of those who had PTSD or depression and also sought treatment, only slightly over half received a *minimally adequate treatment*

Figure 4.2
Top Five Barriers to Seeking Mental Health Care

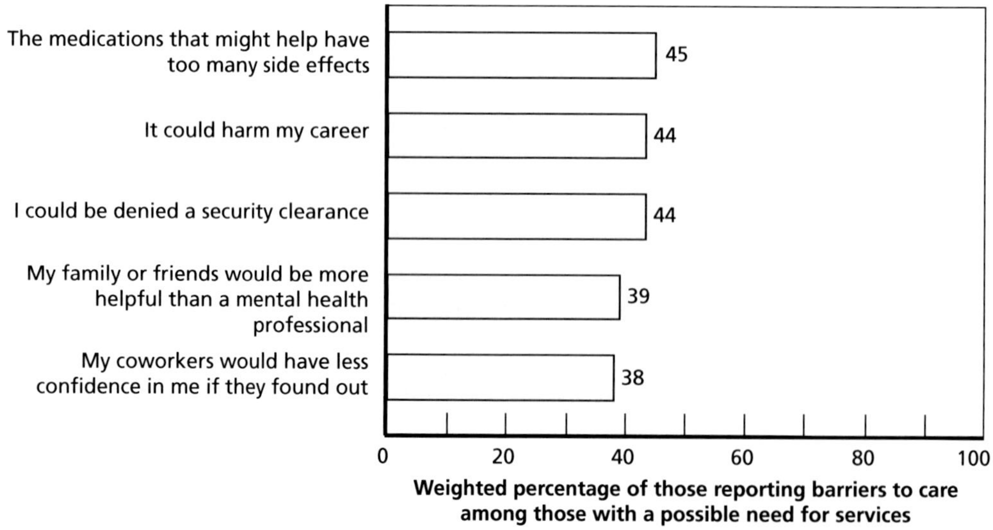

RAND *OP316-4.2*

(defined according to the duration and type of treatment received). The number who received *high-quality care* (treatment supported by scientific evidence) would be even smaller.

The study also identified gaps in the care systems' ability to promote and monitor quality care. In particular, there is room for improvement in the organizational tools and incentives that support delivery of high-quality mental health care. Without these institutional supports, it is impossible to provide oversight to ensure high-quality care, which includes treatment that is evidence-based and also patient-centered, timely, and efficient. DoD and the VA have begun training in evidence-based practices for providers, but these efforts have not yet been integrated into a larger system redesign that values and provides incentives for quality of care.

The VA has been a leader in promoting quality and may provide a promising model for quality improvement of mental health care within DoD. Significant improvements in the quality of care the VA provides for depression have been documented, but efforts to evaluate the quality of care provided within the VA for PTSD remain under way.

Improving Access to High-Quality Care Can Save Money and Improve Outcomes

Unless treated, PTSD, depression, and TBI can have far-reaching and damaging consequences. Individuals afflicted with these conditions face higher risks for other psychological problems and for attempting suicide. They have higher rates of unhealthy behaviors—such as smoking, overeating, and unsafe sex—and higher rates of physical health problems and mortality. Individuals with these conditions also tend to miss more work or report being less productive. These conditions can impair relationships, disrupt marriages, aggravate the difficulties of parenting, and cause problems in children that may extend the consequences of combat trauma across generations. There is also a possible link between these conditions and homelessness. The damaging consequences from lack of treatment or under-treatment suggest that those afflicted, as well as society at large, stand to gain substantially if more of them have access to effective care.

These consequences can have a high economic toll; however, most attempts to measure the costs of these conditions focus only on medical costs to the government. Yet direct costs of treatment are only a fraction of the total costs related to mental health and cognitive conditions. Far higher are the long-term individual and societal costs stemming from lost productivity, reduced quality of life, homelessness, domestic violence, the strain on families, and suicide. Delivering effective care and restoring veterans to full mental health have the potential to reduce these longer-term costs significantly.

Therefore, it is important to consider the direct costs of care in the context of the long-term societal costs of providing inadequate or no care. The RAND study sought to measure the total costs to society by factoring in treatment costs, losses or gains in productivity, and the costs associated with suicide. In addition, the study calculated the cost effect of getting more people into treatment and improving the quality of care.

Estimates of the cost of PTSD and major depression for two years after deployment ranged from $5,900 to $25,760 per case (in 2007 dollars). When these per-case estimates were applied to the proportion of the entire population of 1.64 million deployed service members (as of 2007) that had a probable disorder of PTSD or depression, the study found that the total societal costs of these conditions ranged from $4.0 to $6.2 billion (in 2007 dollars), depending on whether the costs of lives lost to suicide were included.

The cost of TBI was substantially higher per case but varied according to the severity of injury. Estimates of the one-year cost of mild TBI ranged from $27,260 to $32,760 per case (in 2007 dollars); estimates of moderate to severe TBI costs were between $268,900 and $408,520 per case (in 2007 dollars).

There is a high level of uncertainty surrounding the cost of TBI because data are lacking. Based on the study's calculations, the total annual cost associated with the diagnosed cases of TBI (2,776 total cases documented through the middle of 2007) ranged from $591 million to $910 million.

While the costs of these conditions are high, effective treatments for them are available, particularly for PTSD and depression. However, these evidence-based treatments are not yet offered in all treatment settings. The model also calculated the costs associated with PTSD and major depression if evidence-based treatments were more widely available (not enough is known to estimate the effect of improving quality of care for TBI, because there is a lack of long-term research on effective treatment and recovery rates):

- If 50 percent of those needing care for PTSD and depression received treatment and all care was evidence based, this larger investment in treatment would result in cost savings overall (see Figure 4.3).
- If 100 percent of those needing care for PTSD and depression received treatment and all care was evidence based, there would be even larger cost savings. The cost of depression, PTSD, or co-morbid PTSD and depression could be reduced by as much as $1.7 billion, or $1,063 per returning veteran (in 2007 dollars). These savings come from increases in productivity, as well as from reductions in the expected number of suicides.

Figure 4.3
Costs per Case—Including Medical Costs, Productivity Costs, and Costs of Lives Lost to Suicide—That Would Be Saved by Investing More in Evidence-Based Care

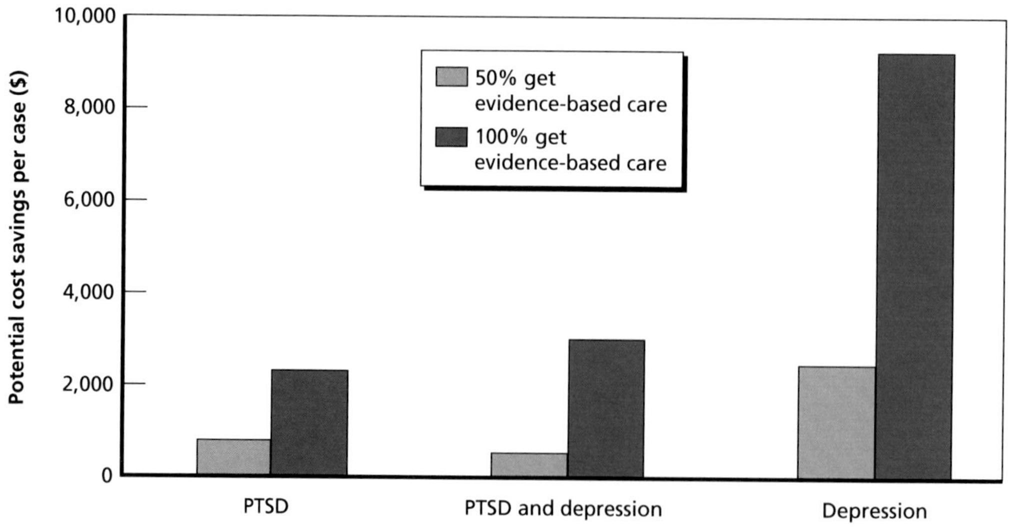

RAND *OP316-4.3*

Given these estimates, evidence-based treatment for PTSD and major depression would pay for itself within two years. No reliable data are available on the costs related to substance abuse, homelessness, family strain, and other indirect consequences of mental health conditions. If these costs were included, savings resulting from effective treatment would be higher.

These results suggest that investing in evidence-based treatment makes sense both to society and to DoD as an employer. Remission and recovery rates would increase, as would retention, work productivity, and readiness of service members and veterans.

Recommendations and Conclusions

Looking across all the dimensions of the analysis, the researchers on this study arrived at four main recommendations for improving the understanding and treatment of PTSD, major depression, and TBI among military veterans:

- *Increase and improve the capacity of the mental health care system to deliver evidence-based care.* There is substantial unmet need among returning service members for care of PTSD and major depression. DoD, the VA, and providers in the civilian sector need greater capacity to provide treatment, which will require new programs to recruit and train more providers throughout the U.S. health care system.
- *Change policies to encourage more service members and veterans to seek needed care.* Many who need care are reluctant to seek it. Service members and veterans need ways to obtain confidential services without fear of adverse consequences.
- *Deliver evidence-based care in all settings.* Providers in all settings should be trained and required to deliver evidence-based care. This change will require implementing systems to ensure sustained quality and coordination of care and to aid quality improvement across all settings in which service members and veterans are served.
- *Invest in research to close knowledge gaps and plan effectively.* Medical science would benefit from a deeper understanding of how these conditions evolve over time among veterans, as well as of the effects of treatment and rehabilitation on outcomes. The United States needs a national strategy to support an aggressive research agenda across all medical service sectors for this population.

Meeting the health care needs of returning troops who have PTSD, depression, and TBI will be challenging. The prevalence of these conditions is high and may grow as the conflicts in Afghanistan and Iraq continue. The systems of care for meeting these needs have been improved, but critical gaps remain. Without effective treatment, these conditions carry significant long-term costs and negative consequences.

Ultimately, this issue reaches beyond DoD and the VA into the general U.S. health care system and society at large. Many veterans seek care through private employer-sponsored health plans and in the public sector. The broader health care system must adapt to the needs of this population if the United States is to meet its obligations to military veterans now and in the future.

AREAS FOR FURTHER STUDY

- How PTSD and major depression evolve over time among veterans.
- How treatment and rehabilitation affect outcomes among the veteran population.
- Whether efforts to support and address psychological health problems and TBI are effective in reducing rates of PTSD, depression, and TBI-related impairments.
- Whether current programs to train providers in evidence-based therapies affect the provision of the quality of care provided to veterans.

5. Called to Duty: The Effects of Deployment on the Earnings of Reservists and How Their Families Coped During the Reservists' Absence

Loughran, Klerman, and Martin, 2006:
Activation and the Earnings of Reservists

Castaneda et al., 2008:
Deployment Experiences of Guard and Reserve Families: Implications for Support and Retention

The extent to which Guard and Reserve forces have been involved in Iraq and Afghanistan is unprecedented in the history of the all-volunteer force.[1] Guardsmen and reservists had been mobilized in earlier conflicts, but not in such numbers. The Department of Defense's (DoD's) "total force" policy, adopted in 1973 with the end of the draft, had reinvented the role of the reserve component, changing it—at least conceptually—from a strategic force for use as a last resort in major-theater wars to one charged with playing a central operational role alongside the active component in many different types of engagements. This shift in role did not materialize in practice, however, until 1991, when almost 250,000 reserve component personnel were activated for Operations Desert Shield and Desert Storm in Iraq (Figure 5.1). Deployments for a series of peacekeeping operations and other contingencies followed during the 1990s, but they were on a small scale compared with deployments to Iraq and Afghanistan.

Not just the number of guardsmen and reservists deployed, but also the characteristics of their deployments have changed dramatically. In the past, with smaller-scale operations, reservists often chose whether to activate; but in Iraq and Afghanistan, more of the activations have probably been involuntary, though there is no explicit information on this. The period of deployment for activated soldiers has often lasted a year or more. Multiple deployments have also been common: About 21 percent of activated guardsmen and reservists had already been deployed more than once between September 1, 2001, and December 2004.

Today's reserve component is both strategic and operational, carrying out a dual purpose made official in 2005 when Congress passed the National Defense Authorization Act. This

[1] The reserve component consists of the Army National Guard, the Air National Guard, the Army Reserve, Navy Reserve, Air Force Reserve, Marine Corps Reserve, and the Coast Guard Reserve. As 2007 drew to a close, more than 550,000 guardsmen and reservists had been deployed to Iraq or Afghanistan—nearly 30 percent of all deployed personnel to that point. In 2004, when fighting was at its heaviest, members of the reserve component made up more than 40 percent of all U.S. troops in Iraq.

Figure 5.1
Activations of Reservists, Fiscal Years 1986–2004

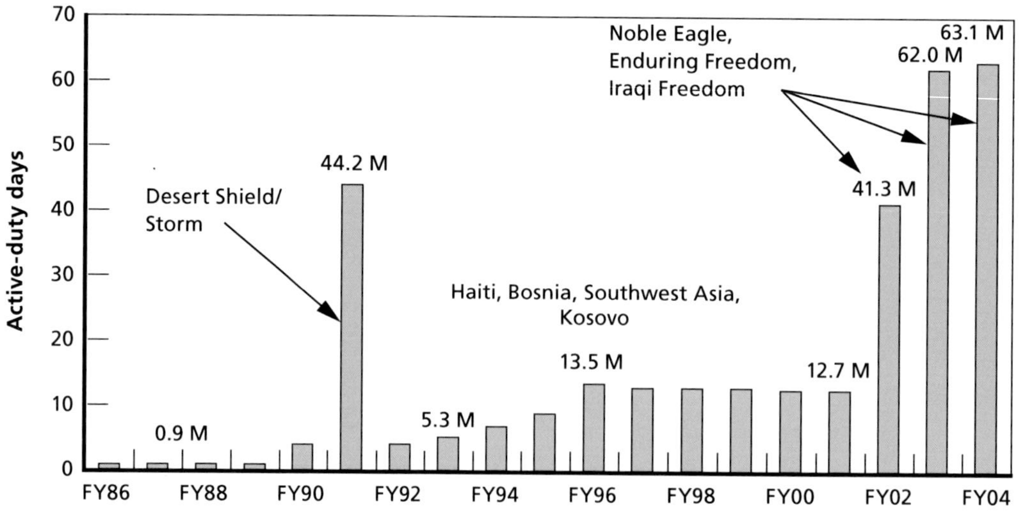

SOURCE: Reproduced from unpublished figures created by Office of the Assistant Secretary of Defense for Reserve Affairs.
RAND *OP316-5.1*

legislation formally called upon the reserve component to contribute to day-to-day military operations instead of serving exclusively as a surplus personnel pool for extended conflicts. Under this new policy, members of the reserve component are fully integrated with the active-duty force and are likely to continue to be called-up at a rigorous pace well into the future.

The new reliance on guardsmen and reservists captured the attention of journalists, who aired a range of concerns about the potential consequences of the heightened role. For instance, a 2005 *NY Times* editorial led off, "If life is unfair ... then military life can be doubly unfair.... But there is one inequity that the federal government should address: the pay disparities for the reservists and National Guard members who have been serving so long and with such sacrifice" ("Part-Time Pay for Full-Time Service," 2005). Press like this shaped a widespread perception that deployments caused guardsmen and reservists to suffer sizable earnings losses. Even some military experts shared this belief, as evidenced by two quotations from military experts interviewed in the Deployment Experiences study:

> Finances are ... a problem. Some families go from an $80,000 salary to a $40,000 salary. Who is going to make up the difference? Sometimes an employer will, but this is not the norm.

> Managing the change in finances is ... difficult. Some families ... are faced with dire financial issues. Trying to manage the change in pay, especially when a family is accustomed to having a certain standard of living, can create stress and other strains on the family.

The study found that these experts tended to mention financial problems more than any other problems facing guardsmen and reservists.

Another fear is that the long, multiple deployments of guardsmen and reservists are taking a particular toll on their families and family life. Deployment causes hardships and challenges even for active-duty families, who expect extended deployments during wartime.

Given the history of the reserve component and the role it played prior to late 2001, guardsmen and reservists could not have anticipated the length of time, far from their families and in harm's way, that they would be called upon to spend. How have these service members and their families coped with these new, arguably unanticipated circumstances? With military operations heavily reliant on guardsmen and reservists, the answer has implications not just for the well-being of the individuals involved, but also for the overall ability of the all-volunteer force to complete its missions.

Have Deployments Caused Reservists to Lose Income?

The concerns about lost income resonate strongly for two principal reasons. The first holds that it would be unfair for reservists, who already make considerable personal sacrifices, to also suffer financial losses because of their service to the country. The second holds that income losses could deplete the overall supply of reservists, leading some members to leave the military earlier than planned, others not to reenlist, and potential enlistees to opt against enlistment.

Substantiation for these concerns came largely from anecdotal evidence cited in the popular press and estimates derived from survey data collected by DoD. These data, drawn from several different surveys conducted between 2000 and 2004, suggest that a sizable number of activated reservists experienced large earnings losses, even before 9/11. Congress appeared willing to act on the basis of these estimates, and various legislative proposals were made to increase the earnings of activated reservists by compensating them directly, offering them tax breaks, or increasing their educational or retirement benefits. In 2006, the National Defense Authorization Act was passed. It contained provisions that would replace the lost earnings of reservists activated for either lengthy (more than 18 months) or multiple deployments.

But the survey data may have been an insufficient basis for new legislation or policy change. Having reviewed this issue in 2004, the Government Accountability Office (GAO) reported several concerns, including the possibility of substantial error and bias in the survey responses, the risk that respondents could have been confused about what to include in their earnings figures (because of an imprecise definition of earnings), and low response rates. The GAO concluded that better information had to be obtained before Congress could accurately determine the need for compensation programs for reservists.

Following the GAO's recommendation, the members of the RAND Activation and the Earnings of Reservists study took a different approach to the issue of reservists' income losses and potential career setbacks. This approach, designed to avoid the problems inherent in the survey data, based its estimates on the precise, well-defined measures of earnings contained in administrative earnings data from the Social Security Administration and DoD's Defense Manpower Data Center from 2000 to 2003. The combined data sets included the earnings for each year of virtually all reservists who served within each of these three years. The RAND team estimated the effects on reservists' income not only during activation, but also in the period after they returned to civilian life.

Overall, the Earnings of Reservists Increase During Deployment

It is much less common for reservists to lose income during activation than the survey-based estimates suggest. In fact, earnings tend to increase. This is because reservists have two sources of earnings when activated: their civilian *and* their military incomes. The overall earnings loss or gain depends on how changes in earnings from both sources work together when a reservist is activated. While the civilian earnings of deployed reservists do decrease substantially, their military earnings increase. This increase in military earnings is double, on average, the decrease in civilian earnings, leading to an overall increase. For reservists activated between 2002 and 2003, for example, civilian earnings dropped by about $9,000. But their military earnings increased on average by about $18,000, causing an overall income gain of about $9,000 during deployment (Figure 5.2).

This is not to say that no reservists lose income. The study team analyzed a sample of reservists who had served zero to 30 days on active duty in 2000 and 30 or more days on active duty in 2002 or 2003. About 17 percent of this group lost some part of their overall earnings. For 6 percent, that loss was more than $10,000; for 11 percent, it was more than 10 percent of their base-year earnings.

Unactivated Reservists Are Even More Likely to Experience an Earnings Loss

Perhaps the most surprising finding was that reservists who are *not* called-up seem to come out worse than their deployed counterparts. Forty percent of reservists who were not activated in either 2000 or between 2002 and 2003 actually lost earnings. Indeed, being activated *lowered* the probability of a reservist losing income by 23 percentage points. This directly contradicts the survey-based findings: Activation may actually be an advantage for reservists in terms of annual income.

Figure 5.2
Average Change in Annual Civilian and Military Earnings for Deployed Reservists, 2002–2003

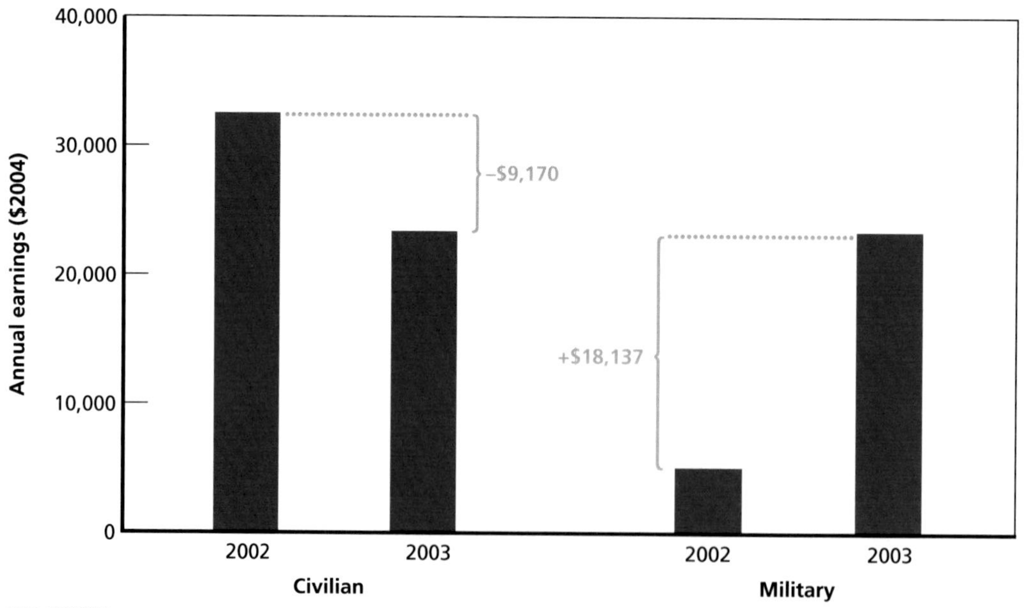

RAND *OP316-5.2*

The Net Increase in Reservists' Earnings Grows Substantially Larger with the Number of Days Deployed

Lengthy deployments were a particular concern among policymakers and the media. But the RAND estimates challenged the basis of fears that reservists lost income because of activation. In fact, the longer the deployment, the greater the increase in the reservist's earnings—in quite substantial increments (Figure 5.3). In 2003, the net increase in annual earnings was 6 percent for reservists serving 31 to 90 active-duty days. That percentage more than tripled for 91 to 180 active-duty days, and it increased by yet another 15 percent for those with 181 to 270 active-duty days. For reservists with the longest periods of deployment—more than 271 active-duty days—annual income changed on net by 56 percent, or almost $20,000.

Why Do the RAND Estimates Differ So Considerably from the Estimates Based on Survey Data?

The RAND estimates have several advantages that likely make them more accurate than the survey-based estimates:

The RAND estimates factor in the value of the tax preference given to military income. The surveys typically instruct reservists to report their pretax earnings. But a sizable share of their military income is tax exempt, which offers an important after-tax advantage. The RAND estimates, in contrast, factor in the value of this tax preference. These estimates indicate that the value of the tax advantage accounts for close to one-third of the average gain in the income of activated reservists.

The measurements in the administrative data are precise. The responses to survey questions are categorical (with each category covering a given income range) and self-reported. Consequently, the measurements they provide of changes in earnings are likely to suffer from sub-

Figure 5.3
Net Change in Annual Earnings in 2002–2003, by Number of Active-Duty Days

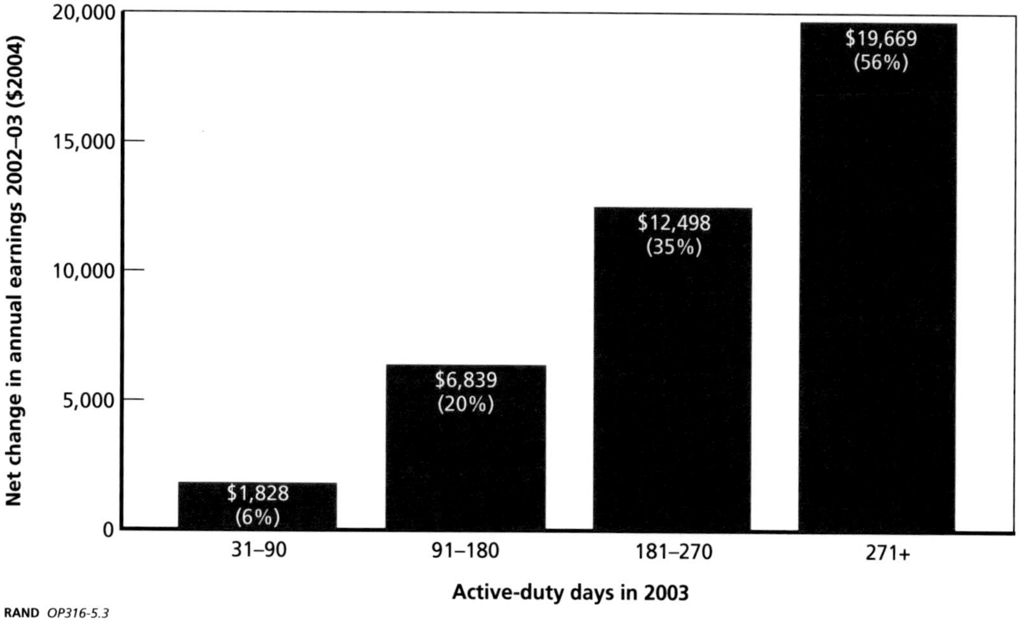

RAND *OP316-5.3*

stantial error and some degree of bias. In contrast, the measurements of earnings in the administrative data are highly precise, with no significant bias.

The administrative data are often more up-to-date. Questions in the 2000–2004 surveys refer to the reservist's most recent activation, which had sometimes occurred several years earlier. Evidence from the administrative data suggests that earnings losses were less common during activations pre-dating the time period in which the surveys were conducted.

The concept of earnings in the RAND calculations is well defined. The concept of earnings used in the surveys is imprecisely defined. Consequently, some respondents may have been confused about what to include in their earnings figures. This concept is very precisely defined in the data used for the RAND calculations.

The administrative data provide a very large sample. Response rates in the surveys were about 30 to 35 percent, raising the possibility that the survey data are unduly influenced by the experience of a select subset of reservists. In contrast, inclusion in the administrative data did not depend on reservists' decisions to respond, but was standard procedure and covered virtually all reservists.

AREAS FOR FURTHER STUDY

- Which types of compensation reforms will help attract and retain reservists most cost-effectively at a time when activation is more likely than ever before?
- What other potential costs might reservists incur from being activated? Monetary costs might include the expenses associated with being away from one's family and possible loss of a spouse's earnings. Non-monetary costs might include risk of injury and the emotional costs of being separated from family and friends.

How Are Members of the Reserve Component and Their Families Coping with the New Pace of Deployment?

In early 2006, David Chu, Under Secretary of Defense for Personnel and Readiness, stood before the newly formed Commission on the National Guard and Reserves. With guardsmen and reservists deploying to Iraq and Afghanistan in unprecedented numbers, Congress had created the commission to recommend needed changes in law and DoD policy to ensure that members of the reserve component would be ready to meet the country's national security needs. In his address, Chu turned the commission's attention to a historically overlooked segment of the military community: the families of reservists and guardsmen. He suggested that military service may put these families through unique hardships and challenges, particularly when faced with lengthy deployments far from home.

DoD has acknowledged that the family issues of *all* service members affect military outcomes. The readiness of families and their quality of life during a deployment influence a service member's performance in the theater and later decisions about retention. In this sense, DoD views family issues as critical to its ability to satisfy the military mission and inseparable from combat readiness. Part of the "new social compact" it announced in 2002 was a commitment to the well-being of military families, aimed at helping ensure mission success, but also at giving back to these families in return for their sacrifices.

Despite the importance of this issue, only a small body of relevant research had been published before 2008. These studies were focused, moreover, almost entirely on active-duty troops and families. This left many unanswered questions about how deployments were affecting reserve component families and how best to support them. Simply applying the research on active component families to reserve component families was problematic in that the two differ in many ways. For example, reserve component personnel and their spouses are older on average; the children of reserve component personnel tend to be younger; the reserve component has a larger percentage of female service members and male spouses; and reserve component families are much more geographically dispersed, tending to live farther from military installations at which they could access traditional family support activities, as well as from other families in the service member's unit.

The Deployment Experiences of Guard and Reserve Families study was a step toward filling this knowledge gap. The core of the research was telephone interviews, conducted in 2006, with respondents from 653 different families—primarily of junior and mid-grade enlisted and junior officers—from the Army Reserve, Army National Guard, Air Force Reserve, and Marine Forces Reserve.[2] The families had experienced at least one deployment outside the continental United States since 9/11. Their interviews provide a rich, qualitative description of their experiences during the conflicts in Iraq and Afghanistan.

The study team supplemented this work by also interviewing military family experts employed by DoD and working for advocacy and support organizations such as the National Military Family Association and the Reserve Enlisted Association. The DoD experts represented each of the department's seven reserve branches and the Office of the Secretary of Defense.

The study aimed at answering three questions:

- What issues do reserve component families face as a result of deployment?
- What are their perceptions of family support resources and to what extent do they make use of such resources?
- How do their experiences and perceptions influence their plans for reenlistment?

The study's analysis grouped responses by family characteristics, shedding light, for example, on whether older spouses and older children had fewer or different needs than younger ones, or whether the families of female personnel experienced deployments differently than those of male personnel. These findings suggest that there are important differences not only between reserve and active component families, but also among reserve component families. They offer basic information that could help DoD tailor support to the needs and experiences of reserve component families.

What Issues Did Reserve Component Families Face?

An activation notice signals dramatic changes in the lives of a reserve component service member and his or her family. The family has to prepare for the service member's departure and cope with his or her absence, and may confront a range of problems directly related to the

---

2 The RAND team interviewed 296 service members and 357 spouses, none of whom were married to each other.

deployment. And there may be benefits as well. The study team delved into all of these issues in their interviews.

Most Respondents Reported That Their Family Had Been Ready or Very Ready for the Service Member's Deployment. Sixty-five percent of the service members and 60 percent of the spouses interviewed reported that their family had been either ready or very ready for their most recent deployment. Only about one-sixth of each group characterized their family as having been not at all ready. In general, older respondents, those who had been married longer, and those with prior military experience were more likely to indicate that their family had been ready.

Yet family readiness can be an elusive concept. DoD formally regards it as "paramount to sustaining mission capabilities and mission readiness" (Office of the Assistant Secretary of Defense for Reserve Affairs, no date) but has no corresponding formal definition of the concept and, by extension, has no measures for assessing how ready a given family may be.

Accordingly, one of the questions the RAND team put to interviewees was how they defined "readiness." No single consistent notion emerged, but approximately two-fifths of the respondents defined it in one of three ways: financial, related to household responsibilities, or emotional or mental. The two groups, service members and spouses, differed as to which definition they chose (Figure 5.4); for example, 58 percent of service members, compared with 45 percent of spouses, defined readiness in financial terms. In contrast, more than half of the spouses defined readiness in terms of emotional or mental readiness, whereas the number of service members that did so was much smaller. Such differences have potentially important implications for the design of support services and policies. Spouses may need more assistance with preparing emotionally or mentally, whereas service members may benefit more from policies that ensure that their families are financially prepared for their deployment.

Figure 5.4
The Three Top Definitions of Readiness, by Service Members and Spouses

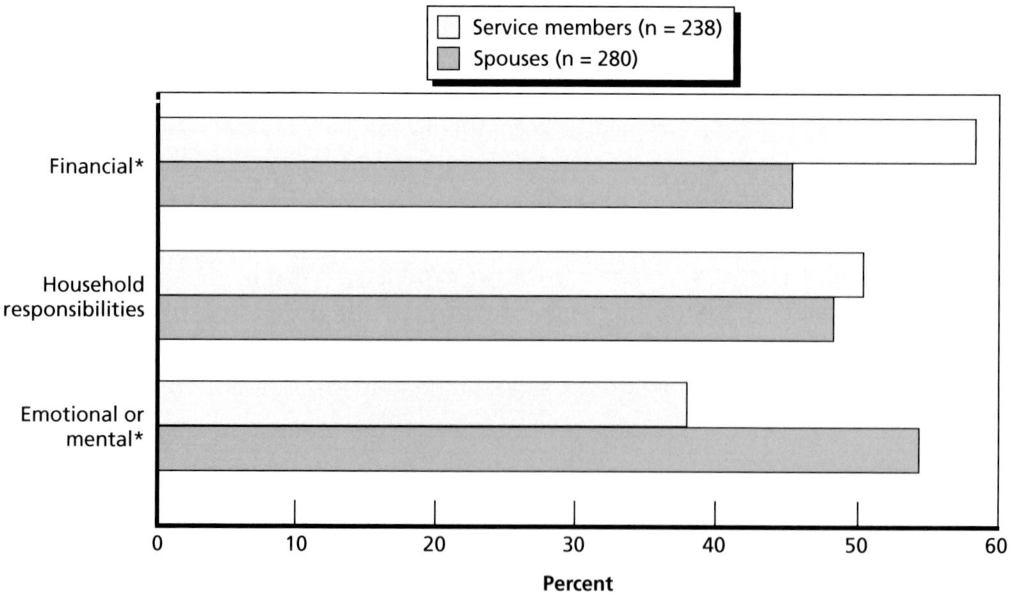

NOTE: Readiness aspects cited by two out of five interviewees.
*Statistically significant at $p < 0.10$.
RAND *OP316-5.4*

Most Respondents Felt Overall That Their Family Had Coped Well or Very Well. Coping was also an ambiguous concept: Only two out of three respondents were able to define it. But despite often not being able to verbalize what it meant, the majority of both service members and spouses felt that their family had coped either well or very well with the most recent deployment (Figure 5.5). The percentage of those who indicated that their family had coped poorly was quite small. Spouses with children, who had been married longer, or who were married to service members with prior active-duty service were more likely to have coped well. Families whose service member had been away longer—especially on a deployment of a year or more—were more likely to cope poorly.

Interestingly, the definitions of coping that interviewees did offer were consistent with the three principal definitions of readiness their responses had identified. Emotional coping and coping with household responsibilities were the most commonly mentioned, and a small percentage of interviewees talked about coping in terms of family finances.

Most Respondents Mentioned Problems Related to Deployment. Four out of five service members and spouses described having experienced problems within the family because of the deployment (Figure 5.6). Personal emotional or mental problems were the most frequently mentioned, followed by problems with household responsibilities, such as difficulties with child care and chores. Children's issues were the third most-commonly described. These included a range of emotional or academic problems and sacrifices children had to make in their deployed parent's absence.

But spouses and service members differed in what they found most problematic and on whether their family indeed had experienced problems. Spouses were much more likely than service members, for instance, to mention the three top problems. Service members, in contrast, were more likely to consider such things as employment and education to have been problems. Most notably, more than two times as many service members as spouses characterized their families as having had no problems at all during the deployment.

Figure 5.5
How Well Reserve Component Families Coped with the Most Recent Deployment

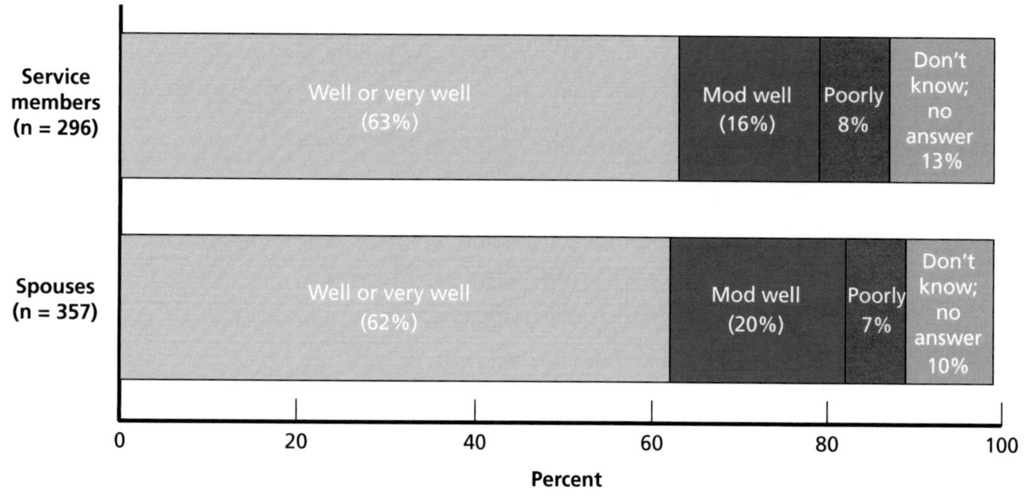

RAND *OP316-5.5*

Figure 5.6
Problems Related to Deployment, by Service Members and Spouses

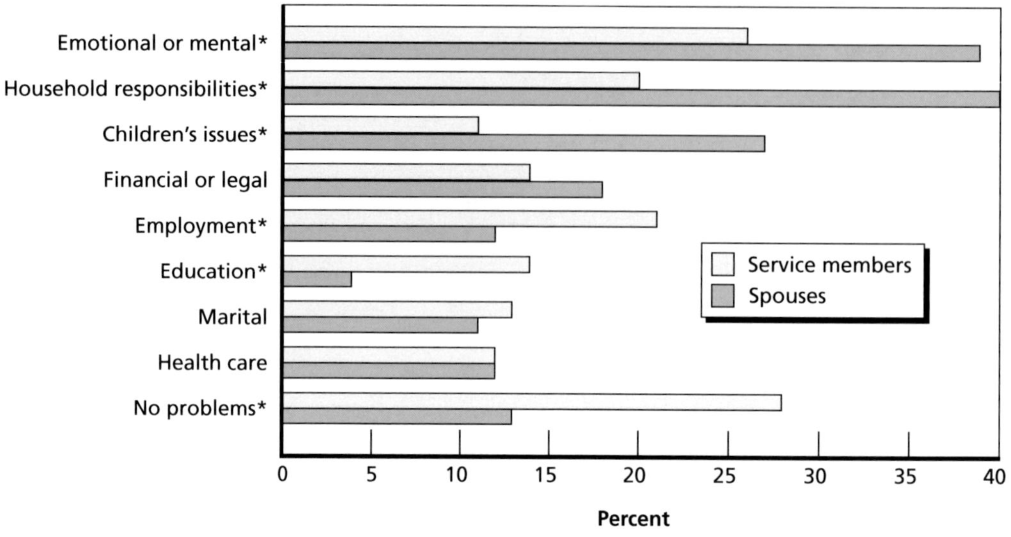

*Statistically significant at $p < 0.10$.
RAND OP316-5.6

Such differences were not limited to service members and spouses. The problems most emphasized by the military experts on reserve component families—financial, legal, and health care—were mentioned by relatively small proportions of service members and spouses themselves. Marital strife, which is popularly believed to be a widespread consequence of deployment, was also infrequently mentioned by service members and spouses.

Most Respondents Also Mentioned That Deployment Had Positive Aspects for Their Family. Despite the difficulties of deployment, reserve component families did experience upsides (Figure 5.7). Many described the deployment experience as having brought their family closer together: This was the most frequently mentioned positive effect. Contradicting the allegation that activated reserve component members suffer earnings losses (and in line with the findings of the RAND Activation and the Earnings of Reservists study), financial gain was the second most-commonly reported upside.[3] Feelings of patriotism, pride, and civic responsibility were another frequently mentioned plus. And roughly 20 percent of interviewees indicated that the deployment had led to an increase in independence, confidence, or resilience for spouses or families at home.

Again, there were differences between the two groups. Spouses were much more likely to mention family closeness; patriotism, pride, and civic responsibility; and independence, confidence, and resilience. In contrast, service members more often mentioned financial gain. Finally, service members were significantly more likely than spouses to report that their deployment had had no positive effects on their families.

[3] Nevertheless, the view that financial losses are one of the costs of deployment appears to be common among guardsmen and reservists: A number of those interviewed did not anticipate their financial gains or considered themselves unusual in accruing them.

Figure 5.7
Positive Aspects of Deployments, by Service Members and Spouses

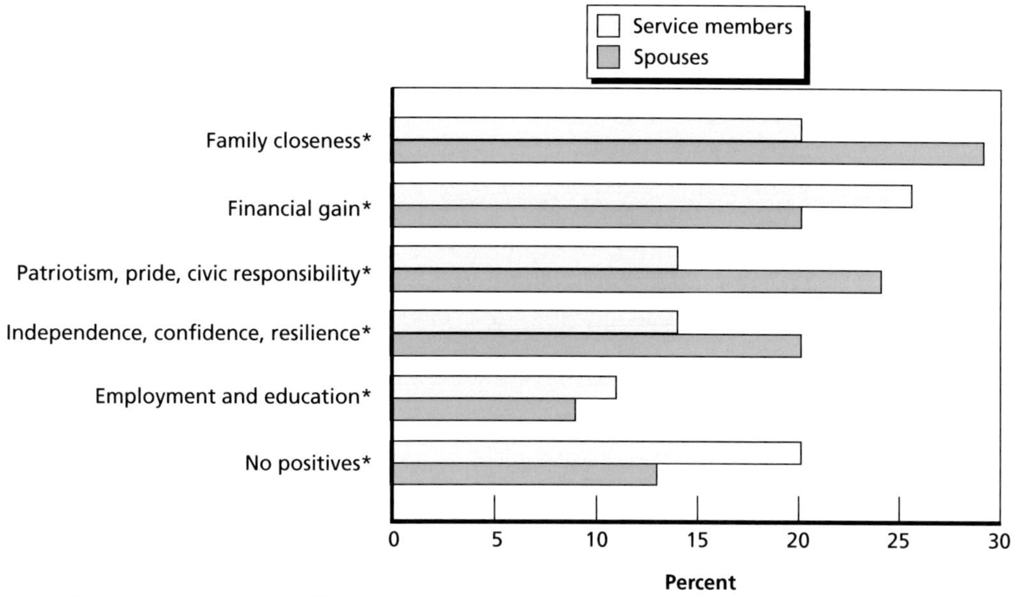

*Statistically significant at $p < 0.10$.

RAND *OP316-5.7*

What Resources Did Reserve Component Families Use During Deployment?

Nine out of ten interviewees reported that their family had turned to either a military or non-military resource during the deployment. Of the military resources, TRICARE, the military's health care program, was the most frequently mentioned. Family support organizations, such as Family Readiness Groups and Key Volunteer Networks, were mentioned nearly as often. Military OneSource, a DoD website that extends online the services military families can access at an installation, came in a distant third.

Among the informal, nonmilitary resources that families drew upon, extended family was by far the most commonly mentioned. In fact, this was the only resource—military and nonmilitary—cited by more than 50 percent of one group of interviewees, the spouses. Some families also turned to religious institutions, and spouses in particular reported making use of friends and neighbors.

What Were Reserve Component Families' Plans for Reenlistment?

Just over half of the service members interviewed indicated that they intended to remain in the reserve component until eligible for retirement, but a large portion—42 percent—expressed plans to leave before that point. These two proportions were repeated closely in the spouses' responses (Figure 5.8). For many service members, their recent deployment had affected their intentions. More than 30 percent of them indicated that the impact had been negative, decreasing their desire to reenlist. But for nearly as many, it had heightened their desire to stay (Figure 5.9).

Figure 5.8
Intention to Reenlist in the Military, by Service Members and Spouses

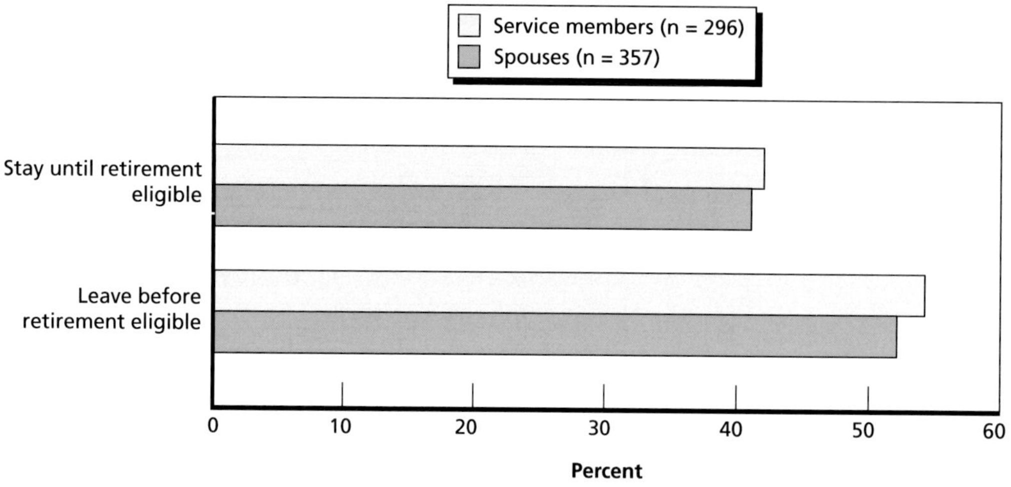

RAND *OP316-5.8*

Figure 5.9
Effect of Deployment Experiences on Service Members' Intentions to Reenlist in the Military

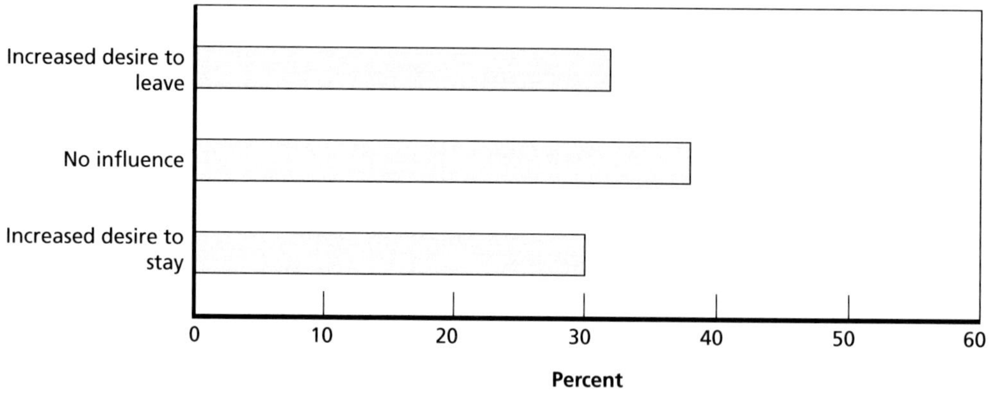

RAND *OP316-5.9*

Their families' experiences during deployment played a significant part in service members' decisionmaking. Those who characterized their family as having been ready or very ready for the deployment, those who believed their family had coped well, and those who mentioned one of the major positive effects—financial gain, increased family closeness, or patriotism and pride—tended to prefer to reenlist. But those whose family had coped poorly or had experienced any of the most frequently mentioned problems were all more likely to make plans to leave.

As for how spouses felt about their partner's military career, there was quite a gap between what service members thought their spouses wanted and what spouses expressed (Figure 5.10).[4] Service members were generally negative about whether their spouses favored their staying in

---

[4] Recall that the service members and spouses surveyed were not married to each other; these were two different samples.

Figure 5.10
Service Members' Impressions of How Their Spouses Felt About Their Staying in the Military vs. Surveyed Spouses' Opinions

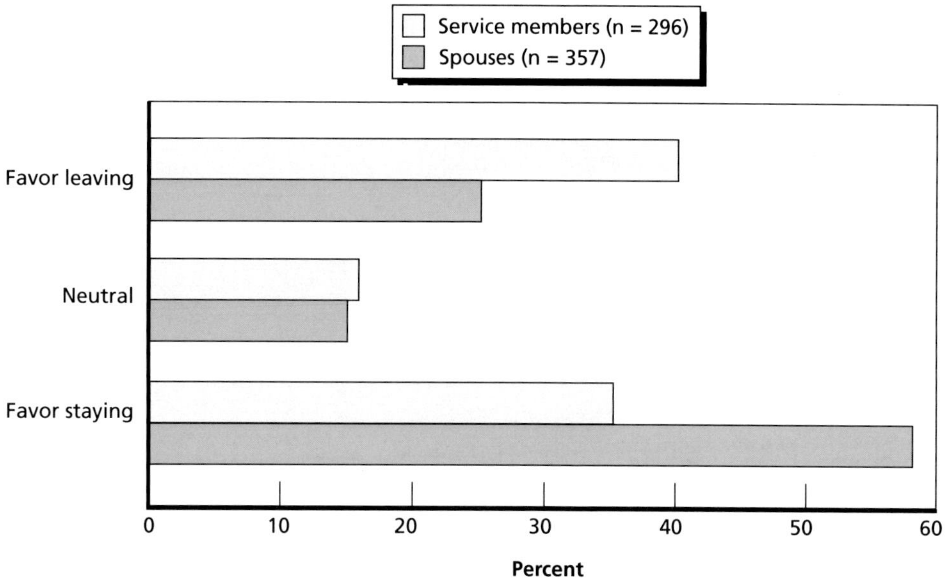

NOTE: Statistically significant at $p < 0.10$.
RAND *OP316-5.10*

the military: Only 35 percent believed their spouse supported their reenlisting. But the spouses who were interviewed were much more favorable, with nearly 60 percent expressing a desire for their spouse to stay in the reserve component.

Constructive Steps in Several Areas Can Improve the Experience of Reserve Component Families During Deployment

It is critical that reserve component families be supported throughout the deployment cycle. Family support can be expected to help support individual performance, mission success, and retention.

The RAND team identified several areas for improvement. DoD policymakers have already begun to implement certain policies and programs consistent with some of the RAND recommendations.

- *Make personnel practices governing deployment more consistent.* Policymakers should seek to make mobilization more predictable in terms of length of deployments and amount of notice given to families. The average deployment should preferably not be more than one year. The amount of notice should be sufficient not only for families to prepare, but also for the military to put all needed supports in place for the whole family.
- *Manage perceptions and expectations.* DoD should manage the expectations of reserve component families so that they are in line with the military's expectations for the frequency and length of deployments. DoD should also find ways to emphasize the positive aspects of being activated, recognizing that family perceptions are sometimes more important than actual experiences.

- *Provide better support and information to families.* DoD's centralized database on reserve component families should be improved so that families can be easily found. Ways to connect families to one another could also be helpful. Recognizing that different families confront different issues during a deployment, information, programs, and efforts to mitigate deployment-related problems should be tailored to the needs of particular types of families. Lessons can be learned from families that experience fewer problems.

AREAS FOR FURTHER STUDY

- The degree to which the findings of this study of 653 reserve component families can be generalized to *all* families in the Army National Guard, Army Reserve, Marine Forces Reserve, and Air Force Reserve.
- The outcomes of any policy changes DoD might make consistent with RAND's recommendations, and their cost-effectiveness.
- Metrics that DoD can use to measure important constructs, such as family readiness and coping, as well as the short- and long-term effectiveness of family support.

6. A Military of Families: How Deployment of a Service-Member Parent Affects Children on the Homefront

Chandra et al., 2010:
"Children on the Homefront: The Experience of Children from Military Families"

Castaneda et al., 2008:
Deployment Experiences of Guard and Reserve Families: Implications for Support and Retention

The professional all-volunteer force has dramatically increased the number of career service members. As a result, the force is slightly older on average than in previous conflicts, more are married (Rostker, 2006, p. 7), and more are parents. In 2006, nearly 1.9 million U.S. children had at least one parent in the military. With the tempo of deployments to Iraq and Afghanistan so demanding, many of these children—particularly those of soldiers and marines—have had that parent deploy, sometimes more than once. Yet little is known about how deployment may affect these children. What is their experience while a parent is deployed and after he or she returns? What types of issues do they face, and how are they coping?

The RAND Children on the Homefront study investigated how the school-age children of service members have been faring academically, socially, and emotionally during the years of war in Iraq and Afghanistan. This study looked at issues faced by military-family children through the lens of both the child and his or her non-deployed parent (or other primary caregiver). The findings were drawn from telephone interviews conducted in 2008 with 1,500 military children, age 11 to 17, and their caregiver parent—in almost all cases, the mother. All of these children had applied to Operation Purple®, a summer camp sponsored by the National Military Family Association to help children from military families—particularly those with a deployed parent—cope with the stress of war. The sample of children used in the study was designed to represent the composition of the deployed force across all four services, the National Guard, and the Reserves. To date, no other study has been comprehensive enough to permit a comparison of the population of military youth with the national U.S. youth population.

The RAND Deployment Experiences of Guard and Reserve Families study, a complement to the Children on the Homefront study, sought to gain insights from interviews of reservists, guard members, and their spouses about how their children have been faring.

Children of Deployed Parents Experience Behavioral and Emotional Difficulties at Rates Above National Averages

Overall, children and caregivers from military families reported having considerably more behavioral and emotional difficulties than have been observed in the general U.S. population (Figure 6.1). Among the military children age 11 to 14, the average score of difficulties was nearly three points higher than the national average. For those age 15 to 17, the gap was even wider, with a difference approaching four points.

Anxiety was a specific problem: About one-third of the military children reported elevated symptoms—double the percentage observed in other child studies (Figure 6.2).

The parents interviewed for the Deployment Experiences study supported these findings. Approximately 26 percent of spouses and 13 percent of service members in the survey reported being concerned that the deployment had adversely affected their children. They mentioned a range of emotional, psychological, behavioral, and academic problems, as well as sacrifices children had had to make, such as having to stop participating in usual extracurricular activities or, in the case of very young children, not seeming to recognize their service-member parent upon his or her return.

The wife of an Army National Guardsman with three children, for example, described a number of difficulties her children confronted:

> There are some problems with the kids, that they are facing, attachment issues. . . . We have a two-year-old who wouldn't sleep in his own bed for the first seven months that [his father] was gone. He wouldn't let me out of his sight. He was scared I was going to leave. Our ten-year-old stopped joining sports, he just wanted to stay home. Stuff like that.

Figure 6.1
Behavioral and Emotional Difficulties Among Military Children vs. Children in the General U.S. Population, Ages 11–14 and 15–17

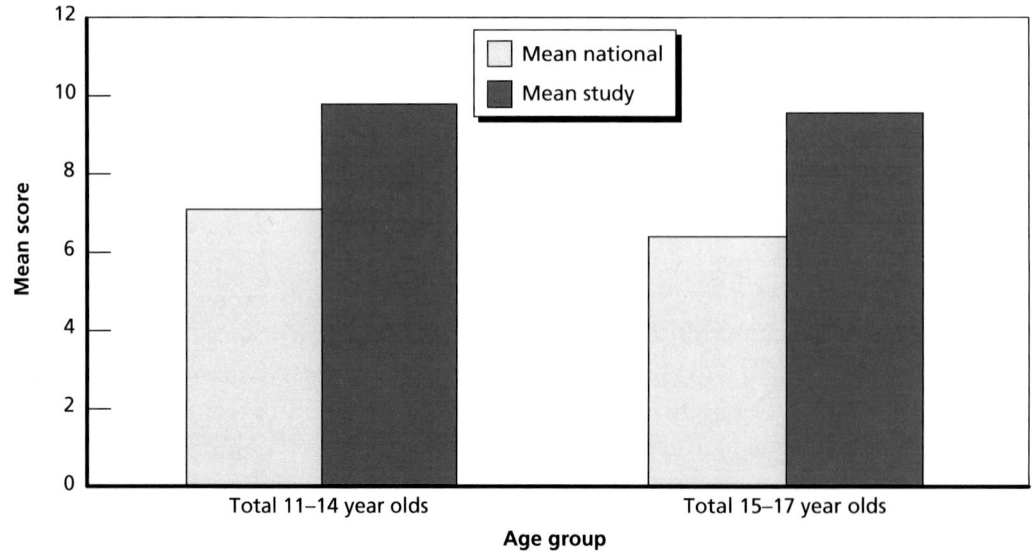

RAND *OP316-6.1*

Figure 6.2
Proportion of Elevated vs. Low Symptoms of Anxiety in Study Sample and Other Child Studies

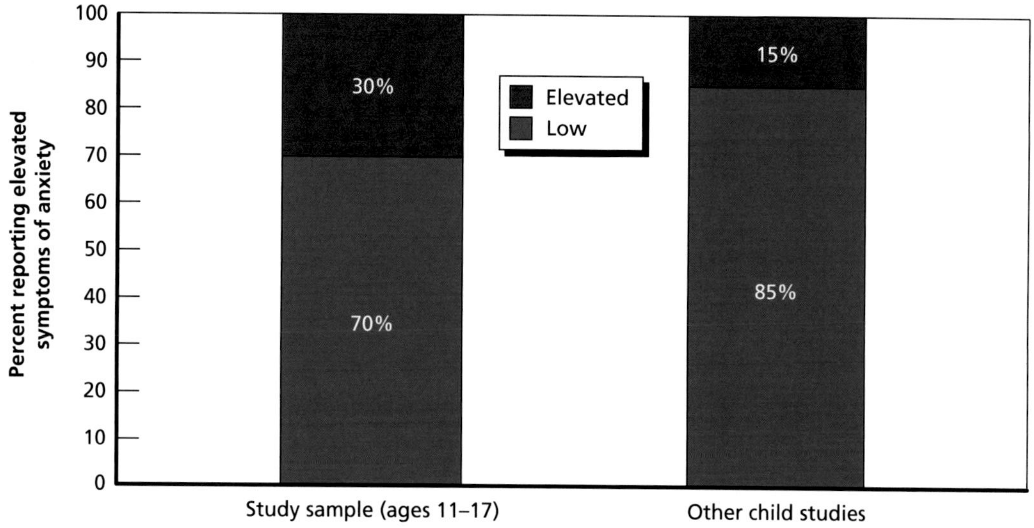

RAND *OP316-6.2*

A female member of the Marine Forces Reserve with two children recounted the difficulties she experienced with her toddler after she returned from duty: "With my child, when I got back I just had to deal with the whole him getting used to me and remembering who I was. . . . I might have seemed like a stranger to him."

Four Factors Put Certain Groups More at Risk

The Children on the Homefront study found that age and gender made a difference in which groups of military children were most at risk for challenges during and after parental deployment, as did the total length of time a parent was deployed and the emotional well-being of the non-deployed parent.

Older Teens Experienced More Difficulties

Older teens had more problems than younger children, both while their military parent was deployed and after he or she returned. At the time of being interviewed, they were having more trouble with school than were younger children and demonstrating more problem behaviors, such as drinking and fighting. Having to take on more household responsibilities, take care of siblings, and miss school activities were all sources of difficulties while the parent was away. After the service member was back home, older children had trouble getting to know their parent again and adjusting to the parent fitting back into the household routine. Dealing with the returning parent's mood changes also posed challenges for older teens.

Girls Reported More Difficulties During Reintegration

The period after the service-member parent returned home was particularly problematic for girls. The most common problems were worrying about the parent's next deployment, dealing with the returning parent's mood changes, and worrying about how parents were getting along.

Longer Total Months of Parental Deployment Were Associated with More Problems for Children

The number of challenges children faced grew as the months of the deployed parent's absence increased. In general, if there was any initial resilience in the early months of a deployment, it appeared to erode over time. The number of deployments was less important than the total months away. These findings held true across the services, in both active-duty and reserve components. This suggests that the stressors of maintaining a healthy home life in the absence of the service-member parent increase in both number and intensity as that parent's time away, as a whole, increases. In addition, longer total away periods may lead to children having more problems re-engaging with the deployed parent upon his or her return.

Children Whose Non-Deployed Parent Reported Better Emotional Health Had Fewer Difficulties

When the non-deployed parent was in good emotional health, children were better able to cope with the experience of deployment and reintegration. They had fewer emotional difficulties, fewer issues with peer and family functioning, and fewer difficulties staying engaged academically and performing well in school.

Several Limitations to the "Operation Purple Camp" Study Should Be Kept in Mind

While the Children on the Homefront study offers previously unavailable insights into the experience of military children, the study did have several limitations. First, the children in the interview sample came from a very specific group: those who applied to attend Operation Purple camp. Accordingly, they and their families may be distinct from others who did not apply. This is a program specifically designed to help children deal with the stress of war. The fact that these children and families were all motivated to apply for this program may be a sign that they were experiencing higher levels of stress around deployment than their peers were. Or, conversely, it could indicate that they were experiencing less stress than their peers, making them better able to do what they needed to apply for the program.

Second, few of the non-deployed parents in the caregiver sample were fathers. Accordingly, it remains unknown whether the deployment experience of military children is different when the mother is the service member and is away from home.

Finally, the interviews were conducted at a particular point in time, so the study did not evaluate the potential impact of a service-member parent's deployment over a period of months or years. This makes it difficult to identify whether the outcomes observed among military children were, indeed, directly related to deployment. A RAND research team is currently collecting longitudinal data for these families that will provide a basis for determining more conclusively how changes in their well-being may relate to deployment.

Interventions Are Needed to Help the Children of Deployed Parents Cope with These Difficulties

Children trying to cope with the absence of a service-member parent are experiencing more emotional and behavioral difficulties than their civilian peers. Consequently, they and their families may need more assistance in addressing their needs. School programming, mental health services, and resources that could be used in the home are all promising approaches to providing that assistance. The findings from the Children on the Homefront study point to several guidelines for intervention:

- Because longer periods of absence seem to lead to greater problems, military families may benefit from support to deal with stressors later in the deployment, rather than only during the initial stages.
- Families in which the non-deployed caregiver is coping with emotional health issues may need more assistance for both the caregiver and the children.
- Because older teens and girls face particular difficulties with deployment and reintegration, they may need targeted support.

DoD and the civilian sector are implementing a number of support programs. Research is needed to evaluate the appropriateness and effectiveness of programs.

AREAS FOR FURTHER STUDY

- The mental health of non-deployed parents (or other caregivers) and the stressors they experience.
- How a military parent's mental health (e.g., PTSD) affects children and the family.
- How the well-being of military-family children changes over time, as deployments start, continue, and end.
- Why girls and older youth have more challenges with a parent's deployment.
- How other family characteristics, such as housing and parental employment, affect children's experience of a parent's deployment.

7. A Few Words in Conclusion

The test to which the Iraq and Afghanistan conflicts are putting the all-volunteer force is far from over. Operations continue in both theaters, with a substantial new surge of troops having deployed to Afghanistan in the early part of 2010. The ability of the force to continue to meet the demands of these and other operations in the future depends on an unbroken stream of new enlistments, good-quality recruits, and high retention rates. In this kind of a career-oriented, professional military, personnel cannot be taken for granted.

Work continues at RAND to illuminate the various effects of deployment on service members and their families, the issues they face, and how policies can be created to address these issues both affordably and effectively. A number of studies now in progress build on the groundwork laid by the research described in this paper. Others take that groundwork in new directions.

Research on the earnings of activated reservists continues, as does work on the experience of reservists' families. One study, for example, is looking at how guard and reserve families reintegrate after a service member returns home. Another examines the employment transitions reservists undergo after having been deployed. A third considers the relationship between pre- and post-deployment health assessments and post-deployment earnings.

The physical and emotional health of service members and their families is another important area of ongoing research. A RAND team is completing a study of state-of-the-art practices for suicide prevention. The effect of deployment on the marital stability of service members is the subject of two new studies that ask whether deployment indeed increases divorce rates, as is commonly believed. An extensive longitudinal study is also under way on the resilience of military families. Jointly sponsored by the Defense Centers of Excellence and the U.S. Army Surgeon General, the Deployment Life study is the first of its kind to follow a cohort of married service members across a full deployment cycle—from a point before they deploy until some time after they have returned home—to observe the positive and negative outcomes that may be associated with military deployments.

Finally, new RAND research is looking at the relationship between disability rating and post-service earnings among veterans.

This growing body of work represents RAND's ongoing commitment to better understand how deployment influences myriad aspects of the lives of today's service members and their families—and by extension, the long-term effectiveness of the U.S. all-volunteer force. Our hope is to provide both decisionmakers and the public with an informed, objective, and comprehensive view of pressing issues and potential solutions, in this way helping to sustain a fighting force that is critical not only to military readiness but also to the ability of the United States to achieve its national security priorities.

References

Castaneda, Laura Werber, Margaret C. Harrell, Danielle M. Varda, Kimberly Curry Hall, Megan K. Beckett, and Stefanie Stern, *Deployment Experiences of Guard and Reserve Families: Implications for Support and Retention*, Santa Monica, Calif.: RAND Corporation, MG-645-OSD, 2008. As of January 25, 2011: http://www.rand.org/pubs/monographs/MG645.html

Chandra, Anita, Sandraluz Lara-Cinisomo, Lisa H. Jaycox, Terri Tanielian, Rachel M. Burns, Teague Ruder, and Bing Han, "Children on the Homefront: The Experience of Children from Military Families," *Pediatrics*, Vol. 125, No. 1, January 2010. As of January 25, 2011: http://pediatrics.aappublications.org/cgi/reprint/125/1/16

Hoge, C. W., C. A. Castro, S. C. Messer, D. McGurk, D. I. Cotting, and R. L. Koffman, "Combat Duty in Iraq and Afghanistan, Mental Health Problems, and Barriers to Care," *New England Journal of Medicine*, Vol. 351, No. 1, July 2004, pp. 13–22. As of January 25, 2011: http://www.nejm.org/doi/full/10.1056/NEJMoa040603#t=articleTop

Hosek, James, Jennifer Kavanagh, and Laura Miller, *How Deployments Affect Service Members*, Santa Monica, Calif.: RAND Corporation, MG-432-RC, 2006. As of January 28, 2011: http://www.rand.org/pubs/monographs/MG432.html

Hosek, James, and Francisco Martorell, *How Have Deployments During the War on Terrorism Affected Reenlistment?* Santa Monica, Calif.: RAND Corporation, MG-873-OSD, 2009. As of January 25, 2011: http://www.rand.org/pubs/monographs/MG873.html

Kavanagh, Jennifer, *Stress and Performance, A Review of the Literature and Its Applicability to the Military,* Santa Monica, Calif.: RAND Corporation, TR-192-RC, 2005. As of January 24, 2011: http://www.rand.org/pubs/technical_reports/TR192.html

Loughran, David S., Jacob Alex Klerman, and Craig Martin, *Activation and the Earnings of Reservists*, Santa Monica, Calif.: RAND Corporation, MG-474-OSD, 2006. As of January 25, 2011: http://www.rand.org/pubs/monographs/MG474.html

Mareth, T., and A. Brooker, "Combat Stress Reaction: A Concept in Evolution," *Military Medicine*, Vol. 150, No. 4, April 1985, pp. 186–190.

Office of the Assistant Secretary of Defense for Reserve Affairs, "Family Readiness," web page, no date. As of January 26, 2011: http://www.dod.mil/ra/html/familyreadiness.html

"Part-Time Pay for Full-Time Service," editorial, *The New York Times*. March 10, 2005. As of January 31, 2011: http://www.nytimes.com/2005/03/10/opinion/10thu3.html?_r=1&scp=1&sq=&st=nyt

Rostker, Bernard D., *I Want You! The Evolution of the All-Volunteer Force*, Santa Monica, Calif.: RAND Corporation, MG-265-RC, 2006. As of January 25, 2011: http://www.rand.org/pubs/monographs/MG265.html

Sollinger, Jerry M., Gail Fisher, and Karen N. Metscher, "The Wars in Afghanistan and Iraq—An Overview," Chapter Two in Terri Tanielian and Lisa H. Jaycox, eds., *Invisible Wounds of War: Psychological and Cognitive Injuries, Their Consequences, and Services to Assist Recovery*, Santa Monica, Calif.: RAND Corporation, MG-720-CCF, 2008. As of January 25, 2011:
http://www.rand.org/pubs/monographs/MG720.html

Tanielian, Terri, and Lisa H. Jaycox, eds., *Invisible Wounds of War: Psychological and Cognitive Injuries, Their Consequences, and Services to Assist Recovery*, Santa Monica, Calif.: RAND Corporation, MG-720-CCF, 2008. As of January 25, 2011:
http://www.rand.org/pubs/monographs/MG720.html